ILLINOIS

Lake Michigan

CHICAGO
Corwith 5.9
McCook
Nerska 5.8
Willow Spr
Argonne
Lemont 2
Romeo 29.3
Lockport 32.7
Joliet 37.5
Plaines 41.5
Drummond 48.2
Lorenzo 52.8
Pequot 57.2
Coal City 58.2
Mazon 66.1
Verona 70.8
Kinsman 74.8
Ransom 79.8
Kernan 84.4
Streator 89.6
Ancona 95.8
Leeds 102.1
Toluca 109.9
La Rose 116.0
Wilbern 120.9
Chillicothe 130.0
Edelstein 138.1
Princeville 144.7
Monica 148.3
Laura 153.5
Williamsfield 158.4
Dahinda 163.3
rg 177.5

Former Santa Fe
Pekin District

AT&SF

TP&W

Former Santa Fe
Peoria Subdivision

TP&W

Gilman 24.6
Piper City 35.0
Watseka 11.1
Webster 4.1
Eftner 61.3E
Kentland 57.1E
Hoosier Lift 38.5E
Reynolds 27.2E
Monticello 21.2E
Kenneth 6.1E
Logansport

TP&W

Chatsworth 40.3
Forrest 47.0
Fairbury 51.8
Chenoa 62.8
Meadows 67.2
Gridley 71.2
El Paso 78.3
Streator Jct.
Cruger 94.0
Pekin Jct. 97.5
Crandall
Morton
Pekin
TP&W
Rawalts 136.8
Canton 139.5
U.E. Siding 146.9
Smithfield 154.5
Kolbe 121.5
East Peoria 108.0
Iowa Jct. 113.9
Bushnell 170.9
Blair Jct. 167.4

INDIANA

P.47 GRAIN ELEVATORS
P.119   "   "
P.151   "   "

C&NW
CC&P ICG
B&OCT-IHB
CC&P ICG
BN CB&Q
AT&SF
McCook
GM Yard
Willow
Springs
B&OCT-IHB
mont

Dearborn Station
C&NW
Union Station
B&OCT
BN CB&Q
BN
B&OCT
Nerska
Bridgeport
Corwith
Yard
IHB
GTW
CHICAGO
21st St.
Jct. and
Coach Yard
iHB
BRC
BRC
GTW
B&OCT
CR
NS
CR
METRA
CSS&SB
BRC
Clearing
Yard
BRC
B&OCT
BRC
CR
BRC
Lake Michigan

NS N&W
GTW
METRA RI
METRA RI
C&WI
B&OCT-IHB
B&OCT
IHB
CSS&SB
GTW
B&OCT
PRR
METRA RI
(IA/S CSX)
NS N&W
IC
UP MP
CSX
B&OCT
UP MP
GTW
(CSX)
CSX

HIGH GREEN
TO MARCELINE

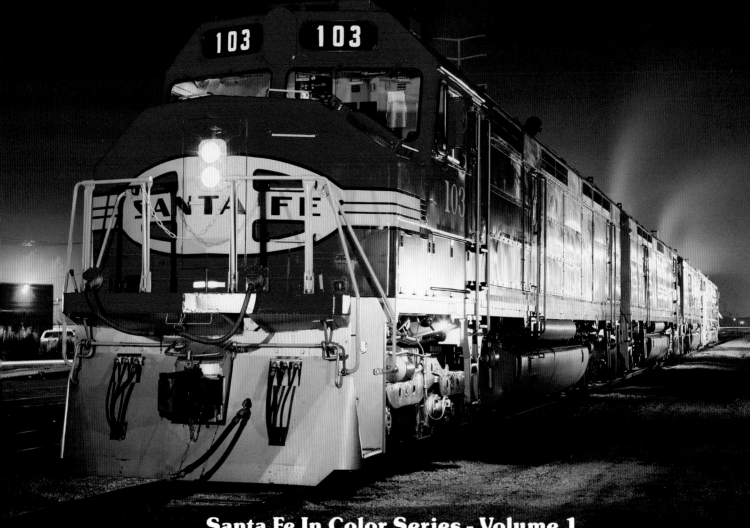

Santa Fe In Color Series - Volume 1
By Joe McMillan
First Printing: November 1989

Front cover and preceding page photo: Super Fleet SDFP45 101 speeds east with train 881 at mile 378 west of Bosworth, Missouri, August 12, 1989. *Jim Primm.* Above: Freshly washed SDFP45's 103, 102, 101 and 100 idle at Chicago's Corwith Yard on Halloween night 1989 before leading a special train to Kansas City the next morning. *Joe McMillan.*

Foreword
HIGH GREEN

The Santa Fe's main line between Chicago and Kansas City has not been exhaustively studied by railroad historians and enthusiasts, even though it is a major link in the national rail network. Perhaps this is due to the absence of notable on-line scenery. The right-of-way follows the contours of obscure Illinois watercourses and slices across the drainage pattern of northern Missouri, and the only mountains it passes are man-made heaps of slag from long-closed mines. Certainly the sights along the way offered scant competition to tournedos of beef with Bearnaise sauce aboard the SUPER CHIEF's diner in vying for the attention of Santa Fe passengers.

Not readily apparent to the casual viewer, though, is the interesting history of Santa Fe's easternmost trackage. The earliest antecedent of the Chicago-Kansas City line was the Chicago and Plainfield Railroad Company, chartered by the state of Illinois in 1859 to connect the towns of its title. Renamed the Chicago, Pekin and Southwestern, the railroad had begun acquiring property along its projected route northeastward from the Illinois River community of Pekin when, in 1872, Chicago promoter and railroad builder Francis E. Hinckley became involved in the project. Hinckley changed the target of the CP&SW construction effort from Marseilles, on the Rock Island, to Streator in order to link up with a Burlington branch leading to Aurora and Chicago. The CP&SW completed its line between Pekin and Streator on January 6, 1873.

Hinckley's ambition was to extend the CP&SW to Chicago and St. Louis, but these goals proved elusive. In 1875, the CP&SW laid track from Streator to Mazon, reaching a connection with the Chicago & Alton. Bankruptcy intervened, however, before the little railroad could grow again. Reorganized as the Chicago, St. Louis & Western, the company finished its line from Mazon to Crawford Avenue in Chicago in 1883-84. This extension, though, failed to convert the "Hinckley Road," as this oft-renamed project was popularly known, into a financial success.

Meanwhile, the executives of The Atchison, Topeka and Santa Fe Railroad had become increasingly concerned as competitors such as the Burlington, Rock Island and Missouri Pacific systems extended their lines past the Missouri River gateways of Kansas City and St. Joseph into the southwest. To respond to these encroachments, Santa Fe management resolved in 1886 to build a new, high-quality line into Chicago and formed the Chicago, Santa Fe & California Railway to pursue this project. A number of routes were considered, but Santa Fe eventually decided to buy the Hinckley Road and construct a new 350-mile line connecting Big Blue Junction, the terminus of the Kansas City Belt eight miles east of Kansas City, with Ancona, Illinois, a point on the Hinckley Road about 100 miles southwest of Chicago. AT&SF officials quietly closed their purchase of Hinckley's line on December 15, 1886 and rewarded Hinckley by making him president of another Santa Fe subsidiary.

Early in 1887, Santa Fe president William Barstow Strong directed Chief Engineer A. A. Robinson to proceed with construction. Having learned much during Santa Fe's period of great physical expansion over the past eighteen years, Robinson and the other engineers were able to plan the course of work in advance, stockpiling materials and stationing work crews along the route to attack the project on a number of fronts. Most of the new line proved easy for Robinson's seasoned forces to build, but the 100 miles between Fort Madison, Iowa and Bucklin, Missouri led through rock ridges left by the passage of glaciers and required a variety of cuts, fills and bridges. More difficult was the problem of spanning the major rivers along the route — the Illinois, Mississippi, Des Moines, Grand and Missouri. Famed engineer Octave Chanute helped Santa Fe design

bridges across these watery obstacles. The Hinckley Road was improved as well with heavier rail and numerous line relocations.

With about 2,000 Santa Fe track workers and 5,000 contractor employees at his disposal, Robinson was able to make quick progress in building the new line during the summer and fall of 1887. By December 31, the track was complete between Chicago and the Missouri River at Sibley. Inclement weather prevented completion of the original Sibley bridge until February 11, 1888, but thereafter only finishing work was needed before the railroad was turned over to the operating department on April 29. Construction of the new line left the Streator-Pekin segment of the Hinckley Road as a branch, which operated as such until its abandonment in 1983.

The Hinckley Road's Chicago terminal facilities, being some distance from downtown, were inadequate for the premium service Santa Fe had in mind. Accordingly, management formed The Atchison, Topeka and Santa Fe Railroad Company in Chicago to build a short extension into the city. This subsidiary teamed up with the Chicago, Madison & Northern, then constructing the Chicago-Freeport line of the Illinois Central, to acquire a joint right-of-way to a connection with the Chicago & Western Indiana at 21st Street. Santa Fe became a tenant of C&WI's Dearborn Street Station, an arrangement which continued through the end of Santa Fe passenger service in 1971.

Over the years millions of dollars were spent on double-tracking the Chicago-Kansas City line, installing signal systems, improving and expanding Corwith Yard in Chicago and ultimately converting that terminal into the busiest piggyback facility in the world. The Chicago-Kansas City line today is a showcase of modern railroading which sees about thirty through trains a day.

For a brief time Santa Fe's presence in Illinois was heightened by its ownership of the Toledo, Peoria & Western, running east from Lomax. The TP&W during the mid-century years functioned as a Chicago bypass for the Santa Fe and the Pennsylvania Railroad, and each company bought a 50% share of the property in 1960. After PRR had been absorbed in Penn Central, though, traffic began to shift to a parallel ex-New York Central branch connecting with Santa Fe at Streator. Conrail had no interest in perpetuating the "Tip-Up," and TP&W was forced to buy the old PRR line from the Indiana border at Effner to Logansport, Indiana in 1976 to maintain an eastern connection with the blue giant. Santa Fe acquired the TP&W's remaining stock in 1981 and sought to maintain the road as a separate operation, but Conrail's decision to drop through rates via Logansport later that year, which diverted virtually all of the remaining through traffic, forced TP&W into a downward economic spiral which could not even be arrested by its formal merger into Santa Fe at the beginning of 1984. Deciding that it could no longer sustain service, Santa Fe sold the Tip-Up's Keokuk branch to the Keokuk Junction in 1986 and the balance of the road to a new company bearing the time-honored TP&W name in 1989.

This book is the first in a series of all-color publications depicting the contemporary operations of the Santa Fe. Although primary emphasis has been placed on presenting the finest in color photography, a special effort has been made to write informative captions providing engineering and historical information not available in previously printed works on the Santa Fe. We hope this book will add to the reader's knowledge and understanding of one of America's premier railroad systems.

— *Michael W. Blaszak*

Left... Dearborn Station, located at Dearborn and Polk (47 West Polk) in downtown Chicago, was home for Santa Fe passenger trains for 84 years. The station was closed in May 1971 with the coming of Amtrak. Passenger trains operating over the Santa Fe were transferred to Union Station at that time and continue to operate out of there. Dearborn Street Station was (and still is) Santa Fe milepost 0.00. Access to the station was provided by the now-abandoned tracks of the facility's owner, the Chicago and Western Indiana Railroad, from 21st Street, a distance of 1.27 miles. The train sheds fell to the scrappers in 1976, but the building itself was spared. Heavily remodeled, it now features trendy shops, law offices, a convenience store, restaurants, a bank and an Ace Hardware store. The interior of the 1885 structure was radically altered, but happily the exterior appears essentially as it has since 1922, when restoration following a fire altered the original roof and clock tower. Dearborn Park, an inner city housing development, now occupies the grounds where the train shed, freight houses and tracks used to be, making a scene like Train 23's departure on October 12, 1967. . . *below* . . . nearly unrecognizable today. *Left, June 1964, Robert P. Schmidt; below, Steve Patterson.*

Above . . . Train No. 9, the KANSAS CITY CHIEF, awaits a 10 p.m. departure for Kansas City behind a pair of General Electric U28CGs. Time is running out for the streamliner. It's April 15, 1968, and in three days the train will be history, another victim of the September 1967 cancellation of the mail contracts by the Post Office Department. Interestingly, during its last decade of operation, No. 9 had no counterpart. Its equipment returned to Chicago on Train 12, the CHICAGOAN. *Below* . . . The last CHICAGOAN arrived at Dearborn Station on time at 8:00 p.m., April 18, 1968, and now, thirty minutes later, Alco RS-1 2395 couples to the rear of the consist to take it to the 21st Street coach yard. *Both photos: Robert P. Schmidt.*

Above . . . It's a snowy Valentine's Day in 1969 as F7A 47C and mates prepare for a 10:00 a.m. departure with Train No. 1, the SAN FRANCISCO CHIEF. The Chicago-San Francisco train and No. 2, its counterpart, would last until Amtrak day, May 1, 1971. (The last No. 1 departed April 30th; the last No. 2 arrived May 2nd.) *Below . . .* Fairbanks-Morse H12-44TS 543 shoves the rear portion of Train 15, the TEXAS CHIEF, into Dearborn in preparation for a 5:20 p.m. departure during March 1968. The TEXAS CHIEF fared somewhat better than Nos. 1 and 2. The Chicago-Houston train became the LONE STAR under Amtrak, but it was discontinued in October 1979. *Above: Steve Patterson; below and SAN FRANCISCO CHIEF track sign: Robert P. Schmidt.*

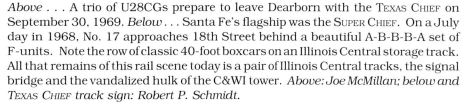

Above . . . A trio of U28CGs prepare to leave Dearborn with the TEXAS CHIEF on September 30, 1969. *Below . . .* Santa Fe's flagship was the SUPER CHIEF. On a July day in 1968, No. 17 approaches 18th Street behind a beautiful A-B-B-B-A set of F-units. Note the row of classic 40-foot boxcars on an Illinois Central storage track. All that remains of this rail scene today is a pair of Illinois Central tracks, the signal bridge and the vandalized hulk of the C&WI tower. *Above: Joe McMillan; below and* TEXAS CHIEF *track sign: Robert P. Schmidt.*

Top left . . . Another set of trains dropped with the coming of Amtrak was Chicago-Los Angeles Trains 23 and 24, the former GRAND CANYON. In better days, Alco PA 74 leads No. 23 out of town on C&WI trackage. The big units were common on this train during their last days. With few exceptions, all 44 Santa Fe PAs were retired in a one-year period between March 1968 and March 1969. The 74 was stricken from the roster on March 13, 1969, and was traded in to EMD for an SD45. *Lower Left* . . . Fourteen months later, No. 23, behind F7 308, is photographed from 18th Street as it departs south along the Chicago River. The tower at the rear of the train is C&WI's 16th Street Tower which controlled entry into the small yard along the river. *Above* . . . The engineer and conductor of No. 15 compare notes before departure while carmen couple connections between the engines and train. U28CGs 357, 352 and 351 will do the honors up front today. Note the Lee work clothes advertisement on the Franklin Building across the street from Dearborn. The sign has appeared in the background of countless photographs of Dearborn Station over the years. Although quite faded, the sign was still readable in 1989! *Top left: January 10, 1968, David DeVault; Lower left: March 1969 and* GRAND CANYON *track sign: Robert P. Schmidt; above: July 23, 1968, Joe McMillan.*

There's probably no better place to view trains in Chicago than from Roosevelt Road, just south of Union Station. If you were standing there on May 13, 1971, two weeks after the birth of Amtrak, you would have seen . . . *top right* . . . a very long, Santa Fe-looking Amtrak SUPER CHIEF/EL CAPITAN pull out of Union Station behind five F-units. *Bottom right* . . . Four years later, Amtrak SDP40Fs 504 and 511 lead the LONE STAR at the same location. At left a departing Burlington Northern commuter smokes up Taylor Street while Amtrak No. 347, the ILLINOIS ZEPHYR, waits with BN commuters to back into the station. In May 1975 . . . *above* . . . the 516 pilots the LONE STAR out of town while low clouds float across the Sears Tower and downtown Chicago. Notice the changes in the city skyline during this four-year period: In 1971 the Sears Tower had not been built, and the huge Pennsylvania Railroad freight house was still standing. In the later views, a few truckloads of rubble are all that remain of the freight house and the just-completed 110 story Sears Tower dominates the skyline. *Three photos: Joe McMillan.*

Santa Fe maintained a large coach yard at 21st Street and Archer in Chicago. Amtrak leased the facility in June 1976 and serviced trains there until its own facility near Union Station (on the site of the old Pennsylvania Railroad coach yard) was completed in 1981. The coach yard was closed in June 1981 and, in 1989, was in the process of being sold to two Chinese American development groups. (The 21st Street facility was located across from Chicago's Chinatown.)

Amtrak received its first order of EMD SDP40Fs in June and July 1973. The first thirty units (500-529) were assigned to Santa Fe and the next ten (530-539) to Burlington Northern. Units 528 and 529, however, bounced back and forth between Santa Fe and BN, as the need dictated. *Above* . . . Nearly new Amtrak 521 and 512 are serviced at 21st Street in September 1973. Seventy-four leased Santa Fe F-units powered passenger trains on the railroad during the early days of Amtrak. With the arrival of the SDP40Fs, the last of the F-units were reassigned to freight duties, making their last run in Amtrak service on the West Coast on August 1, 1973. *Left* . . . In December 1971, the 311C and Super Chief/El Capitan consist are towed through the car washer at the coach yard. *Top right* . . . Enroute to 21st Street in June 1975, a smoky Santa Fe GP7 nearly obliterates the Chicago skyline as it leaves Union Station with a Southwest Limited consist. *Below right* . . . The "21st Street Chief" brings an Amtrak coach to Union Station in July 1974. The BN commuter yard, seen above the switcher, has since been completely renovated by Metra, Chicago's commuter rail agency. The Crooks Terminal Warehouse, another one of those familiar Chicago landmarks that has appeared in rail photographs over the years, was torn down in 1988. *Above and below right: Joe McMillan; left: Allen W. Clum; top right: Robert P. Schmidt.*

Old age was creeping up on the Santa Fe passenger F-unit fleet by early 1973, resulting in repeated delays to Amtrak's SUPER CHIEF. Santa Fe, tired of the situation, unilaterally replaced the F-units on the train with F45s, an F-unit booster and a steam generator car for steam. The unusual power consists were replaced in mid-1973 with the arrival of the new Amtrak SDP40Fs. *Above* . . . On April 15, 1973, F45s 5920, 5914 and a booster lead No. 4 into Union Station. *Below* . . . Every year several Illinois railroads band together to operate an "Operation Lifesaver" special. The specials usually make a day trip out of Chicago in the spring, stopping at various communities enroute to promote grade crossing safety. In May 1987, Santa Fe and Amtrak teamed up to operate the annual outing from Chicago to Galesburg and back. Here, freshly painted SDFP45 5998 and Amtrak F40PH 381 lead the 7-car special out of Union Station. *Above: Paul C. Hunnell; below: Michael W. Blaszak.*

Corwith Yard, located about six miles southwest of downtown Chicago along Interstate 55, is Santa Fe's primary freight facility. Today, the large yard is dedicated to the handling of piggyback trailers and containers. The 128-acre intermodal facility—called "Checkpoint Chico"— is a busy place. An average of 25 intermodal trains arrive and depart each day. In 1988, the facility set a new record by loading and unloading 532,673 trailers and containers, an average of one trailer or container every minute. The railroad maintains six Drott Travelift overhead cranes and two huge LeTourneau Letro-Porter container side loaders to load and unload intermodal freight. Thirty-three radio-equipped "hostler tractors" are used to spot trailers trackside, or move them to parking areas. A drive through Checkpoint Chico reveals many interesting trailer slogans and logos, a few of which are displayed here. It goes without saying that intermodal traffic is what today's Santa Fe is all about. *Seven photos: Joe McMillan.*

Santa Fe has taken delivery of its new locomotives at Corwith for many years. EMDs are interchanged to the railroad at McCook via the Indiana Harbor Belt, while GEs usually come through Belt Railway of Chicago's Clearing Yard from the Norfolk Southern. At Corwith, radios are installed and the new locomotives are inspected, fueled, sanded and powered up for revenue service. *Top left* . . . Brand new GE U33C 8507 idles on the 4th of July, 1969. *Above* . . . Just delivered Santa Fe GP39-2 3611 shakes hands with new Amtrak SDP40F 646 at Corwith on August 24, 1974. Santa Fe transported SDP40Fs from McCook to Amtrak's 16th Street facility where they were placed in service. The 646 would be assigned to the Seaboard Coast Line at Miami, Florida. *Left* . . . On a cold, bright day in January 1985, brand new 6410 sits at the head of a string of just-delivered GE B23-7s. This was the fourth and last order for these 2250 h.p. locomotives. In June and July 1988, Santa Fe received twenty 4000 h.p. GE Dash 8-40Bs numbered 7410-7429. On July 1, the 7420 and three sisters wait to be placed in service at Corwith. The company received its second order of these interesting locomotives (7430-7449) in April 1989. *Top right* . . . Also delivered in 1988 were twenty GP60s: 4000-4019. The first three pose in numerical order on the service tracks beside the Corwith enginehouse on May 28. *Bottom right* . . . Santa Fe took delivery of several batches of Southern Pacific and Cotton Belt GP40-2s and GP60s in 1984 and 1988. The units were placed in service by Santa Fe and run to Kansas City where they were delivered to the Cotton Belt. GP60 9616 awaits its first call to service on April 26, 1988. *Six photos: Joe McMillan.*

In addition to newly delivered locomotives, Corwith sees its share of demonstrators. In June 1974 the Stanray Corporation imported a 1250 h.p. diesel hydraulic switcher from Romania in hopes of interesting US railroads in this exotic power. Nicknamed the "Quarter Horse," the little off-centercab unit arrived on the Santa Fe in July. Technicians spent several days working on the engine in the Corwith enginehouse . . . *left* . . . prior to its entering service. After some body damage was repaired and new paint applied, the switcher went to work shunting cars . . . *below*. The Quarter Horse made a round trip to Kansas City, but spent most of its time in Chicago. The quiet-running switcher was deemed too light for Santa Fe service, especially when braking long strings of cars. By September 1974 the demonstrator was working on the Southern Railway in Chamblee, Georgia. It bounced from railroad to railroad, but two years later it was back in Chicago switching for the Soo Line at Schiller Park. The "Horse" eventually became No. 78 on the roster of the Washington Terminal Company, Washington, D.C. *Three photos: Joe McMillan.*

In 1986 Santa Fe hosted EMD GP60 demos 5, 6 and 7. The three squeaky clean, blue and white units are shown
. . . *above* . . . pulling out of the yard onto the main line at Corwith Junction (mile 6.1) with train 199 (Chicago-
Richmond, Calif.) on April 23, 1986. The company was impressed with the performance of these three locomotives
and later took delivery of forty GP60s in two orders: 4000-4019 in 1988 and 4020-4039 in 1989.

Pulaski Road is a fine location from which to photograph Santa Fe trains leaving Chicago. Parking is available just
off the bridge, and afternoon or morning light is great. It also offers an opportunity to view Santa Fe's entry into
Chicago. Corwith Yard is situated perpendicular to the main line to the right of the photograph. The portion of the
train just entering at right is crossing the Stevenson Expressway, Interstate 55. The signal bridge on the curve (under
the "WCKG" sign) is the home signal for an Illinois Central (formerly GM&O) crossing. The crossing is guarded by
IC's Corwith Tower and is occasionally an operational headache for Santa Fe switching activities. Santa Fe's double
track main line disappears in the background at the left of the photo. The main line used to begin at 21st Street,
mile 1.23, but in 1982 both mains were abandoned from there to Bridgeport (mile 3.1) where the rails cross the South
Branch of the Chicago River. Both tracks were removed between the two points, but the City of Chicago later used
the right of way to construct its Chicago Transit Authority rapid transit line to Midway Airport. Amtrak's SOUTHWEST
CHIEF and an occasional switch move are the only activity today on the main tracks beyond Corwith Junction. Empty
TOFC/COFC flats are often stored on one of the main tracks. At Bridgeport, Amtrak switches to IC tracks to reach
21st Street, then curves across the Chicago River on Amtrak trackage into Union Station. For all practical purposes,
Santa Fe's main line to Texas and California begins right here at mile 6.1. *Four photos: Joe McMillan.*

In November 1987, the Grand Trunk Western Railroad began running its intermodal trains 204 and 205 into and out of Corwith Yard. Westbound 205 entered the south end of Corwith on the AT&SF-GTW connection. Santa Fe's piggyback yard unloaded GTW's trailers and made up eastbound 204. This arrangement, however, ended in June 1988. GTW power continued to enter Corwith with direct interchange traffic until March 26, 1989 when that, too, was stopped. During this time, GTW power was serviced by Santa Fe and laid over at Corwith during the day. *Above* . . . GTW GP40-2 6405 and GP38-2 6221 (both ex-DT&I units) wait for their assignment on April 28, 1988, as Santa Fe GP20 3063 (sold in February 1989 to the new TP&W Railroad at East Peoria) and mates are serviced. *Below* . . . Two months later, another GTW consist suns itself in the afternoon sun at Corwith. Freshly painted GP38-2 5705 is ex-Missouri Pacific 2044, part of an ongoing GTW program to replace GP9s with refurbished ex-MoPac units. Note the Sears Tower between the Santa Fe and GTW locomotives in both pictures.

Canadian National SD50F 5456 visited the Santa Fe in October 1988 to give company officials and employees an opportunity to inspect its new state-of-the-art desk-top control console and other features of the "wide cab" design pioneered by CN. The big unit made a round trip from Chicago to Fort Madison on October 13th and a round trip to Los Angeles between October 17 and 22. Santa Fe will acquire 40 EMD GP60Ms and 60 GE B40-8s in 1990, all equipped with the "comfort" or "wide cab." The tour of the CN SD50F helped members of Santa Fe's Cab Redesign Committee formulate cab design plans for its units. On a rainy October 17 morning . . . *top left* . . . CN 5456 waits on the Corwith ready tracks beside GE Dash 8-40B 7424. Later. . . *bottom left* . . . the CN unit leads the Q-NYLA out of the yard at 11:15 a.m. for Los Angeles. Trailing the 5456 are SDF40-2 5259 (ex-Amtrak SDP40F 633), SDFP45's (remanufactured FP45's) 5995, 5993, 5998 and business car MOUNTAINAIR. *Four photos: Joe McMillan.*

21

Top left . . . A snowy February 4, 1988 finds a westbound intermodal leaving Corwith approaching Pulaski Road behind GP30 2785, GP39-2 3694 and GP30 2750. The 2785 is formerly TP&W 700, acquired through merger with that railroad on January 1, 1984. *Bottom left . . . A* year earlier SDF45s 5954, 5977 and C30-7 8056 pump up air on train 168 after making a double over. As the train prepares to leave, GP7 switcher 2005 and mate scoot alongside. In February 1986, San Bernardino shops began remanufacturing SD45-2s. The first thirty were painted in the merger red paint scheme and numbered 7200-7229. When the Southern Pacific and Santa Fe merger was denied in July 1986, the red paint stopped flowing, and the remaining 36 SD45-2 rebuilds emerged in blue and yellow with numbers 5830-5865. Units 7200-7229 were renumbered 5800-5829 between August and November 1986. *Above . . .* On April 29, 1986, the 7204, 7205, 7206 and 7210 lead train 199 out of Chicago. In just over two weeks, unit 7205, the second locomotive in this consist, would be involved in an accident at Barstow, California. It would be released from the shop in August 1986 as blue and yellow 5805. *Three photos: Joe McMillan.*

Above . . . On November 17, 1973, U25B 6613 and a U33C speed westbound freight by McCook station, mile 12.8. Santa Fe purchased 16 U25Bs in 1962 and 1963. Numbered 1600-1615, the 2500 h.p. units spent most of their lives running between Chicago and Kansas City. They were renumbered 6600-6615 in 1969 and 1970, and were off the roster by April 1979. McCook station was destroyed by fire on July 7, 1986 and was torn down three days later. *Right . . .* SD45 rebuild 5402 wheels train 199 in April 1987 at Lawndale Avenue, just east of McCook. The 5402 was the third Santa Fe locomotive to receive merger red and yellow paint, but it became the prototype for the rest of the fleet. The paint on the first two red units, 5394 and 5401, was modified to match the 5402. *Far right, top . . .* Four merger red units lead 1st 199 at First Avenue in McCook on June 4, 1987. The skeletonized track at the left of the train is used by maintenance of way forces to load machines on flat cars. F*ar right , bottom . . .* A few minutes later, 2nd 199 behind SD40-2 5140 is about to clatter across the B&OCT/IHB at McCook. That's the First Avenue overpass in the distant background. *Four photos: Joe McMillan.*

Willow Springs, located at mile 17.4 will soon be a very important station on the Santa Fe. For years the company served a large General Motors stamping plant from its GM Yard, located off the main line between miles 15 and 17. The GM plant is shutting down, but on March 19, 1989, United Parcel Service announced that it would build a $150 million facility on the site. UPS's huge building, consisting of 1.3 million square feet (nearly 30 acres) will be the world's largest package sorting facility. Santa Fe's GM Yard will be converted to a piggyback terminal handing approximately 90,000 trailers annually. The new facility is expected to open in late 1993 or early 1994. Long before the excitement of the UPS announcement . . . *top left* . . . Amtrak's CHIEF roars through Willow Springs enroute to Union Station. The Chicago to Los Angeles CHIEF ran only during the summer of 1972, from mid-June to mid-September. The Willow Springs station was being used by maintenance of way employees at the time, but was torn down about 1980. *Bottom left* . . . No. 17, Amtrak's SUPER CHIEF/EL CAPITAN with six passenger F-units up front speeds across the Des Plaines River at Lemont in 1971. *Above* . . . On July 3, 1973, the same train, now numbered 3 and name shortened to SUPER CHIEF, rounds the big curve at Lemont (mile 25) behind SDP40F 510, making its first run. *Left page, three photos: Robert P. Schmidt; above: Joe McMillan.*

*Below. . . Me*rger red SD45-2 5709 guides train 199 over the Des Plaines River at Lemont (mile 24.4) at 5:02 p.m. on a cold winter day in February 1988. *Top right* . . . A few hundred feet further west (mile 24.7), GE Dash 8-40B 7423 heads the Q-NYLA across the Chicago Sanitary and Ship Canal. The date is March 25, 1989. The "mail train," as the Q-NYLA is called, consists of U. S. Mail and UPS trailers and is one of Santa Fe's hottest trains. Much of the traffic originates on the east coast and trails Conrail's TVLA right into Corwith yard. When the train comes to a stop, the CR power cuts off, cars are switched in and out of the consist, Santa Fe units couple up and the train leaves town. *Bottom right* . . . Several local freights serve industrial areas between Chicago and mile 51 west of Joliet. On a bright day in February 1979, one of them has nosed into a snow bank at Lemont while the crew has lunch. Later, the local will back out, cross over to the north track, back to mile 24 and enter the Argonne Industrial spur to switch several customers. *Below: Steve Cigolle; right, two photos: Joe McMillan.*

Top left . . . In March 1988, Santa Fe began running a dedicated double-stack train for Hyundai Merchant Marine Company of Seoul, Korea. Santa Fe and Conrail team up to handle the once-a-week run between Los Angeles and Croxton, New Jersey. Train 148, the westbound stacker, usually leaves Chicago on Saturday afternoons. The schedule, however, depends upon ship arrivals and is subject to change. On Saturday, June 11, 1988, train 148 races into Lockport at 3:33 p.m. behind C30-7 8083. *Bottom left . . .* U33C 8513 leads eastbound mixed freight by the Lockport station (mile 32.7) on May 27, 1979. Both the Lockport and Lemont stations were closed on January 22, 1982 and were both torn down in January 1984. *Above . . .* U23B 6320 leans into a curve under Lockport's 9th Street bridge in September 1981 with roadswitcher R-IL041 (roadswitcher, Illinois Division), more commonly referred to as the "041" local. The train originates at Joliet and works the heavily industrialized corridor east of there. The 6320 was retired in June 1983 and traded to General Electric for an order of C30-7s. *Four photos: Joe McMillan.*

One of the best Santa Fe photo spots in the Chicago area is the Division Street overpass in Lockport (mile 33.3). Division Street used to lead to a swing bridge across the Chicago Sanitary and Ship Canal, but that structure was removed, making this location a very quiet and peaceful place to watch and photograph trains.

Above and below . . . On May 3-7, 1986, Santa Fe officials operated a 33 van RoadRailer test train between Chicago and a General Motors plant at Van Nuys, California, and back to Chicago. Santa Fe management approached the Brotherhood of Locomotive Engineers and the United Transportation Union prior to the running of the test train asking them to cooperate in the operation by using two-person crews and skipping intermediate crew change points. The unions balked at the idea and the railroad, anxious to run the train, decided to do so with supervisory, non-union personnel. As the train journeyed west, the unions called a strike against the railroad, which lasted until the test train arrived back in Chicago. The GM test train is shown speeding west in early morning light on May 3rd. Trailing GP50 3821 are business cars MOUNTAINAIR and SANTA FE, and a RoadRailer transition/tool/sleeping car. *Two photos: Joe McMillan.*

Above . . . SF30C 9541 (a remanufactured U36C) leads train 113 under Division Street on February 13, 1988. The Chicago to Kansas City train will make a set out/pick up at Joliet before continuing west (see page 39). *Below* . . . Freshly painted GP30 2703 brightens an otherwise dark, gloomy day in February 1984 with an eastbound "high and wide" special for one of the Chicago area refineries. *Two photos: Joe McMillan.*

Division Street is also a handy spot to photograph new locomotives making their first revenue runs. *Above* . . . Brand new GE Dash 8-40Bs 7420, 7418, 7416 and 7410 are on train 198, Friday, July 1, 1988 at 6:44 p.m. These four are part of a twenty-unit order (7410-7429) received in June and July. Twenty more (7430-7449) arrived in April 1989. *Right* . . . Nearly a month earlier, at 4:12 p.m., June 4, 1988, spotless GP60s 4005, 4004 and 4003 make their first run at the point of train 148, the Saturday-only Hyundai double stacker. The three Canadian-built GP60s were delivered the previous day and placed in service at Corwith. The company acquired twenty GP60s (4000-4019) during May and June and twenty more (4020-4039) in July and August 1989. Forty red/silver "comfort cab" or "wide nose" GP60M versions are due in mid-1990. *Two Photos: Joe McMillan.*

Lockport's Division Street is the most convenient location in the Chicago area to photograph Santa Fe trains in fall colors. *Above* . . . GP30 2755 is on a local, October 12, 1985. On the same day . . . *top right* . . . two EMDs and two GEs pilot train 168 (Chicago-Los Angeles). *Bottom right* . . . U36C 8773 leads mixed freight at the same location on a dark day in September 1978. The 8773 was remanufactured at Cleburne shops in May 1986, emerging as merger red SF30C 9545. *Above and bottom right: Joe McMillan; top right: Mike Danneman.*

Top left . . . On February 13, 1988, westbound train 168 skirts the Des Plaines River at mile 35.3 as it passes the east end of Joliet Yard. That's the Lockport Locks in the background, the second of eight locks on the 333-mile Illinois Waterway connecting Lake Michigan with the Mississippi River. *Bottom left* . . . Two months later, GP38-2 2378 (formerly TP&W 2009) and GP20 3045 switch Joliet Yard before leaving with the "041" local to serve industries east of town. That's the main line of the Elgin, Joliet & Eastern Railway in the foreground. *Above* . . . Train 301 (Kansas City to Chicago) switches the east end of Joliet Yard under EJ&E's Des Plaines River lift bridge. Trailing GP20 3069 are GP30 2772, GP7 2015 and, not shown, red GP30s 2748 and 2776. Date: May 9, 1987. *Below* . . . SF30C 9541 eases train 113 across the old canal turning basin (mile 36.4) at the west end of Joliet Yard while picking up a long string of cars. The 200-foot bridge is unusual in that it is built askew on a sharp curve. *Four photos: Joe McMillan.*

Above . . . On a beautiful afternoon in May 1982, C30-7 8123 leads a westbound across the long-abandoned Illinois and Michigan Canal at mile 36.5, just west of Joliet Yard. In the locomotive consist is a switcher deadheading to Kansas City for maintenance. The Des Plaines River flows quietly by in the foreground. *Above: Joe McMillan.*

Joliet Union Depot (mile 37.5) is a popular place for train watchers. It has always been a busy location, and still is today. In 1989 the visitor can watch 10 weekday Amtrak trains, 30 weekday Metra commuter arrivals/departures (formerly Rock Island and ICG), as well as freight trains of the Santa Fe, Illinois Central, Chicago, Missouri & Western, Chicago Central & Pacific, Iowa Interstate and CSX Transportation. To eliminate grade crossings and "controversies with street cars," the tracks were elevated through downtown Joliet in a mammoth project during 1910-1912. JUD was built as a part of that project and was owned by the railroads it served. The station now belongs to Metra (which inherited Rock Island's one-third interest) and the City of Joliet (which purchased its two-thirds ownership from the Santa Fe and Illinois Central Gulf). In 1989 the structure was undergoing extensive restoration.

Above . . . FP45 5943 and F45 5923 pause at Joliet with the SAN FRANCISCO CHIEF on November 1, 1970. GP38 3543 eases by the passenger with a westbound freight. *Below, right* . . . Train 168 with units 5055-5035-7200 (SD40-2/ SD40-2/SF30B) eases by JUD at the prescribed 25 m.p.h. at 10:58 a.m., September 2, 1989. *Below, left* . . . The time-table board inside JUD, January 18, 1975, shows the Amtrak lineup at the time. *Left, below and timetable board: Joe McMillan; above: Robert P. Schmidt.*

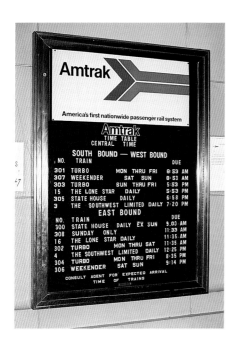

For many years the Santa Fe and Illinois Central Gulf (formerly Gulf, Mobile & Ohio) shared paired trackage between Plaines (mile 41.5) and Pequot (mile 57.2). Westward trains used Santa Fe rails (north track) and eastward trains used ICG's (south track). Traffic over the 15.7-mile section is governed by automatic block (ABS) signals meaning trains cannot operate against the current of traffic without special authority. (Most of the Chicago to Kansas City route is operated under CTC rules, which allows trains to run in either direction on either track as desired by the dispatcher.) In later years, maintenance on the ICG track did not meet Santa Fe standards and orders were issued slowing trains through the section. Concerned about the situation, Santa Fe purchased the south track from the ICG in April 1986 and rebuilt it. Much of the section is located in wooded areas with limited access, but operations are interesting. While Santa Fe now owns both tracks, Amtrak trains that operated over the Illinois Central Gulf (Chicago to St. Louis) prior to the sale still have trackage rights and are frequently routed over the Santa Fe between Joliet, Plaines and Pequot. Illinois Central retains trackage rights from Joliet to Millsdale, mile 45.5, to serve an industry on a spur off the south track. At mile 51, Santa Fe serves several chemical plants on a spur off the north track. The "051" local out of Joliet spends much of its time here. There are other industrial spurs at Drummond, mile 48.2, and Blodgett, mile 50.3, which primarily serve military ordnance depots.

Probably the most photogenic location on the Plaines-Pequot section is the twin bridge over the Kankakee River at mile 52, just east of Lorenzo. *Left* . . . Neighborhood kids play as SDF45 (remanufactured F45) 5961 leads train 165 across the 645-foot structure. *Above* . . . SD45 5391 rounds the curve at MP 51.7 with train 199 at 5:18 p.m., May 20, 1988. *Below* . . . Three months later, at 12:25 p.m., August 28, 1988, the 9532 and 5377 (SF30C/SD45) rumble across the Kankakee River with 13 cars of mail and UPS on the Q-NYLA. *Above and left: Joe McMillan; below: Steve Cigolle.*

Above and right . . . It's July 1969 and, due to a IC maintenance project on the south track between Pequot and Plaines, trains are being routed over the north track. A temporary train order office has been set up at Pequot and the operator is handing up orders to Train 16, the TEXAS CHIEF. *Top left* . . . Santa Fe's Coal City depot (mile 58.2) is shown in 1969 while still an open agency. The station, located just a mile west of Pequot, still stands in 1989, but is used only by maintenance of way forces. *Middle left* . . . A number of station names were dropped from the Eastern Region timetable effective May 21, 1989, and shortly thereafter, maintenance of way crews began removing the signs. The Drummond, Kinsman and Ransom signs lie in a materials yard near the Coal City depot. *Bottom left* . . . In August 1973, passenger F-unit 307 speeds westbound freight through Coal City. The warbonnets had been removed from Amtrak service earlier that summer and reassigned to freight duties. They would be a common sight on Illinois Division freights for a year or so. The 307 was retired the following month and sent to Cleburne shops in Texas for conversion to CF7 2538. It now serves the MidSouth Rail Corporation in Mississippi and Louisiana as its 7012. *Five photos: Joe McMillan.*

Scenery along the Santa Fe between Coal City (mile 58.2) and Streator, mile 89.6, is rather uninteresting, unless you are fond of corn fields. The track is nearly level and relatively straight, allowing for fast running (passenger: 79 m.p.h. and freight: maximum of 70 m.p.h.). The frame depot at Mazon (mile 66.1) still stands in 1989, but like the Coal City station, it is used only by maintenance of way personnel. Probably the most interesting photos on this portion of the railroad are those taken from the Illinois Highway 170 overpass (mile 79.2) at Ransom. *Top left* . . . The early morning light glints off train 188 at Ransom at 6:36 a.m., May 14, 1988. *Bottom left* . . . A year earlier, Amtrak No. 3, the westbound SOUTHWEST CHIEF, speeds by the same location at 6:37 p.m. with a consist nearly split between head-end and passenger cars. *Above* . . . SD45 5615 leads a train of mixed freight eastward through Ransom in October 1976. The 5615, later remanufactured and renumbered 5379, remains in service in 1989. *Two photos, left: Joe McMillan; above: Jim Primm.*

Streator, Illinois, mile (89.6) was for many years an interesting railroad town. It seems the city was once covered with railroad tracks. In addition to the Santa Fe, the town was served by the Wabash (later N&W), Gulf, Mobile & Ohio (later ICG), Chicago, Burlington & Quincy (later BN) and New York Central (later Penn Central, then Conrail). Streator is on Santa Fe's main line, but it was on branch lines of the other roads. Streator is still a worthwhile place to visit, but the number of railroads is down to three: Santa Fe, BN and CR. Streator was also Santa Fe's terminal for trains assigned to the Pekin District (Ancona to Pekin). *Above* . . . Photographed from the Broadway Street overpass, Amtrak Train No. 16, the LONE STAR, pauses at Streator in May 1979. Interestingly, the lead locomotive, SDP40F 526 was later acquired by the Santa Fe, remanufactured, and is today SDF40-2 5255, one of 18 former Amtrak passenger units on the roster (5250-5267). *Below* . . . The same train departs town with business car MOUNTAINAIR in tow. The large Owens-Illinois glass container plant dominates the background. Amtrak trains still stop at Streator in 1989, but the station is no longer manned. Santa Fe maintenance of way people occupy portions of the structure. *Two photos: Joe McMillan.*

Above . . . You're aboard the lead locomotive on Santa Fe Train No. 15, the TEXAS CHIEF at Streator on July 17, 1969. On the point today are a pair of 350 class GE U28CGs and a U30CG. No. 15 was due out of Streator at 6:55 p.m. *Below* . . . Five years later, Amtrak's version of the same train, the LONE STAR, pauses at Streator before continuing west. *Two photos: Joe McMillan.*

For many years Streator has been an important interchange between the Santa Fe and the New York Central, and NYC successors Penn Central and Conrail. Trains between the two roads have been interchanged since the mid-1960s, but true run-throughs didn't begin until 1968 when a connecting track was built from the NYC trackage along Livingston Road in the south part of town to Santa Fe's south main track at mile 91.5, about 1.9 miles west (geographically south) of the depot. *Above* . . . Conrail 2710 and 3663 (U23B-GP35) ease to a stop for a crew change near Conrail's mobile home office in Streator on October 21, 1978. The N&W crossing in front of the locomotive has since been removed. Below . . . Santa Fe unit coal train C-KCSR blasts by Conrail milepost 145, six miles east of Streator at 4:18 p.m., May 10, 1986, behind SD40-2s 5090, 5097 and D&RGW SD40T-2 5365. The train originated on the Rio Grande at Converse, Colorado and was interchanged to the Santa Fe at Kansas City, then to Conrail at Streator. It is enroute to the Northern Indiana Public Service Company at Wheatfield, Indiana. *Two photos: Joe McMillan.*

Above . . . Conrail GP40 3194 leads train 288 off the connecting track onto Santa Fe's south main track at 10:38 a.m., May 10, 1986. The grade crossing behind the train is Livingston Road which parallels the connection part way to Conrail's office. *Below* . . . On the Fourth of July, 1988, train 362 with Conrail GP38-2 8166 and two Santa Fe units on the point pause for a crew change at Iowa, as Conrail calls its Streator office. The train is nearly a solid consist of empty auto racks returning east for loading. The frequency of run-through trains has varied over the years, but in 1989 there were about two trains each way daily. *Two photos: Joe McMillan.*

One of the best photo locations in the Streator area is Santa Fe's crossing of the Vermilion River at mile 91.7, just a few hundred yards west of the Conrail connection on the south edge of town. Illinois State Route 23 crosses over the railroad at the west end of the bridge giving the photographer an unusual perspective. *Above* . . . At 9:50 a.m. on a beautiful morning in May 1988, GP39-2 3418 approaches the highway 23 overpass as it leads train 301 around the curve at mile 92. Train 301 is a main line local. *Left* . . . A year earlier, a westbound local crosses the Vermilion River behind B23-7 6406. *Right* . . . Train 199 crosses the 307-foot structure at 6:32 p. m., May 14, 1988. *Above and right: Joe McMillan; left: Mike Danneman.*

Above . . . Train 851 zips by the abandoned location of Moon, Illinois (mile 93.9) at 7:55 p.m., May 7, 1988, as the last fragment of sun sinks beneath the horizon. Leading the eastbounder is SF30C 9524.

Ancona (mile 95.8) features a long curve that bends the main line through 55.5 degrees of curvature. It was also the junction with the Pekin District, which was Santa Fe's only branch line in Illinois prior to its abandonment in July 1983. The best photo location is probably at the rural highway crossing at the south edge of town, or at the timber trestle over Prairie Creek. *Top right* . . . It's a cold afternoon in January 1977 as GP20 3167 waits on the big curve at Ancona for an opposing westbound to cross over to the north track. Twelve years later, at 3:35 p.m. on April 15, 1989 . . . *bottom right* . . . Conrail SD50s 6772 and 6749 lead run-through train 213 westbound toward a 2:40 a.m. arrival in Kansas City. The big EMD's will leave Kansas City at 3:40 p.m., April 16th with eastbound run-through train 302. *Three photos: Joe McMillan.*

Before continuing west on the main line, let's travel the Pekin District. The line played an important part in Santa Fe's entry into Chicago from Kansas City. Named the Hinckley Road after its promoter, Francis E. Hinckley, the dilapidated Chicago, Pekin and Southwestern Railway built northward from Pekin toward Chicago in the early 1870s. Funds ran out before its dreams were realized, however, and the road fell into financial hardship. Santa Fe, interested in quickly completing its Kansas City to Chicago line in 1886, saw in the CP&SW (by then renamed the Chicago & St Louis) a route into Chicago and an opportunity to save nearly a hundred miles of construction. The Santa Fe purchased the C&StL in December 1886 and connected its line from Kansas City to it at Ancona a year later. The Santa Fe rebuilt the railroad from Ancona to Chicago and began operating through trains between Chicago and Kansas City on April 29, 1888. AT&SF operated the Ancona to Pekin portion of the old C&StL until it was abandoned in July 1983.

The Pekin District was always susceptible to heavy drifting during winter storms. The line saw infrequent traffic and was angled perpendicular to prevailing winds, which could cause heavy drifting with moderate snows. Santa Fe had managed to keep the line open in previous winters by using a Jordan spreader, but heavy snows in January 1977 pushed the spreader to its practical limit. When big drifts piled up again in January 1979, Santa Fe called out heavy artillery in the form of rotary plow 199361. This was only the second time the plow had been used since it was constructed at Topeka shops in 1959 from an old steam locomotive tender and parts from a retired rotary. *Above* . . . The big machine bites into a moderate drift at mile 18 on the outskirts of Benson. *Bottom left* . . . Earlier in the day the work train stops at Minonk (mile 13) for lunch. Two GP20s are assigned to the plow this day. The unit directly behind the snowplow provides current to operate the plow's rotary blade, while the second GP20 furnishes traction to push the two along. *Top left* . . . It's late in the day as the train approaches mile 28 where plowing will stop. Snow depth is not deemed a problem beyond that point. The work extra will return to Streator this evening. It's January 22, 1979, and it's been a long day. *Three photos: Joe McMillan.*

On April 26, 1969, the Railroad Club of Chicago teamed up with the Santa Fe to operate the "Chico Chief," a one day, round trip excursion between Chicago and Pekin. F7A 308L, F7B 306A and two coaches made up the special. The 308L was later renumbered 345L and converted to CF7 2464 in 1977. It now serves the Columbus & Greenville Railway out of Columbus, Mississippi as their 802. The booster became the 353A, but it was heavily damaged by fire in May 1977 and sold for scrap later that year. *Above* . . . The excursion pauses on the N&W diamond at Crandall (mile 43.4) for photos. *Top right* . . . The "Chico Chief" poses for another photo opportunity, this time at Streator Junction (mile 30.7). Santa Fe trains operating over the Pekin District had trackage rights over the TP&W from this point west to Pekin Junction, a distance of six miles. *Bottom right* . . . Later in the day, the special loads up at Pekin for the trip back to Chicago. *Three photos: Joe McMillan.*

Above . . . CF7 2448, GP9 2278 and CF7 2474 have an unusual Pekin District assignment on September 2, 1980. Early that morning the company had received a Ringling Bros. and Barnum Bailey circus train from the Chicago & Illinois Midland Railway at Pekin. Santa Fe will handle the train to Chicago where it will be interchanged to the Milwaukee Road for the trip to Milwaukee, Wisconsin. *Below* . . . The Streator to Pekin local behind GP20 3049 passes by the station sign at Cooper, Illinois (mile 41.0), and later . . . *right* . . . pauses at Morton (mile 45.7) on March 2, 1983. *Three photos: Michael W. Blaszak.*

Above . . . U23B 6333 pauses during switching chores at Pekin on September 16, 1978. *Left* . . . A GP7 lays over at Pekin's East Yards in February 1974. The 75-foot turntable, moved here in 1917 from Emporia, Kansas, was once bordered by a five-track round-house. The Streator-Pekin local rumbles south out of Benson . . . *below* . . . on January 10, 1981. GP38 3551 and B23-7 6363 lead the 10 car, 700-ton train. Note the TOFC equipment behind the units; Morton had an active piggy-back ramp at the time. *Above and left: Joe McMillan; below: Michael W. Blaszak.*

The date is July 7, 1983 and this is the last Streator to Pekin local; the Pekin District would be abandoned the next day. The 3503 (renumbered two years later to 2303) and caboose 999172 are headed for the end of the line to retrieve several empties. *Bottom right* . . . The 3503 and waycar amble through Roanoke. *Above* . . . At 2:01 p.m., the short train sails through a sea of green just south of Morton. Thirteen minutes later . . . *top right* . . . the local rounds a curve at Groveland, Illinois. Pekin is only 10 miles away. *Three photos: Michael W. Blaszak.*

Back to the main line. There are no curves in the 14.1 miles between Ancona and Toluca, but there are plenty of corn fields. Toluca (mile 109.9) is a small, friendly town in Marshall County. A visitor entering the village on State Route 116A is greeted with this sign . . . *top left*. Shown on the sign is a Santa Fe train and a huge pile of tailings from a long-abandoned coal mine, called the "jumbo" by local residents. The city fathers of Toluca certainly had the right idea when it came to naming streets . . . *far left*. A visit trackside in 1969 . . . *bottom left* . . . would have revealed an open station, an amenity that would last less than a year. The structure was torn down in the early 1970s. Years later, in July 1988 . . . *middle left* . . . the C-SRKC blasts through Toluca with Colorado-bound coal empties behind a set of Rio Grande motors. The D&RGW power added some variety to the Illinois Division, but there was only one train set assigned to this run, which made the train an infrequent visitor. The contract has since expired and the train no longer operates. *Above* . . . One is rewarded with a commanding view of the flatlands from atop the jumbo pile. If you had made the steep climb on April 15, 1989, and were there at 10:06 a.m. you would have seen train 991 speeding east through town behind GP60 4013, two GP50s and Dash 8-40B 7420. The speedster left Richmond, California at 4:04 a.m. April 13 and will arrive at Corwith yard this morning at 11:55. *Toluca welcome sign: Mike Danneman; all others: Joe McMillan.*

At La Rose (mile 116.0), six miles west of Toluca, Santa Fe's double track main line enters a wooded region and begins its descent to the Illinois River at Chillicothe. The tracks follow Crow Creek from just west of Toluca to the river, crossing it eight times. Illinois Route 89 passes over the tracks at mile 117 and is a good vantage point from which to photograph eastbound trains in the morning. Be careful of passing highway traffic, however. *Left* . . . GP9 2256 leads a main line local at mile 117 on May 18, 1985. The air is full of black smoke and fluffy cottonwood seeds. A year earlier . . . *above* . . . a pair of Conrail SD40-2s (6450-6476) round the same curve with a run-through train. *Below* . . . Exactly fifteen minutes later, Amtrak No. 4 glides into view behind a pair of F40PHs. *Three photos: Joe McMillan.*

One of the most scenic areas along the Santa Fe in Illinois is the Illinois River valley, roughly from mile 117 to 138. On the east side of the river, Wilbern (mile 120.9) is especially notable. The tracks form an "S" curve through the tiny town, and two rural roads pass over the rails nearby, one east of town at milepost 120 and the other west of Wilbern at mile 122.8. Each offers good vantage points from which to view or photograph trains. The west bridge is wide and has little vehicular traffic. It is an excellent place to spend the day. The best photos at this location are of eastbounds in the morning. Wilbern is also a great place to photograph fall colors. *Top left* . . . SDFP45s 5998, 5993 and 5995 lead Hyundai double-stack train 148 through Wilbern on October 22, 1988 at 3:20 p.m. The three six-axle F-units had arrived at Chicago earlier that morning after making a round trip to California behind Canadian National SD50F 5456 (see page 20). The smoke stack in the background belongs to an abandoned Sinclair Refining Company pipe line pumping station, one of several along the Santa Fe in the area. *Bottom left* . . . Caboose 999193 trails a westbound at mile 123 on a beautiful fall day in October 1978. A decade later it would be unusual to see a caboose behind an intermodal train. *Above* . . . On the same day, an eastbound piggybacker (left) behind 5599 and 5049 (SD45/SD40-2) speeds by a Conrail run-through trailing Santa Fe 6312 and CR 3014 (U23B/GP40). The trains are about to cross Crow Creek (mile 120.3). This view was taken with a long lens from the bridge at mile 120. *Top left: Steve Cigolle; above and bottom left: Joe McMillan.*

The vantage point from Wilbern's east bridge (mile 120) is good for viewing both east and westbound trains. To get to the structure, turn south off Illinois Route 17 onto Washburn Road (also called Tax School Road) several miles west of the intersection with Route 89. *Top left* . . . A westbound local crosses Crow Creek at mile 120 behind the 6393, 6328 and 6389 (B23-7/U23B/B23-7). Tagging along are 33 loads, 16 empties and caboose 999170. It's 3:12 p.m., May 12, 1984. *Bottom left* . . . Four years later, another mainline local, train 301, approaches Wilbern at mile 121.5. Four axle power is the norm for these trains, but today SD40-2 5125 is up front. *Below* . . . Well worn B23-7 6386 and three mates lead another train 301 east through "downtown" Wilbern at 9:08 a.m., July 4, 1988. *Three photos: Joe McMillan.*

Above . . . "Go for it" states the graffiti on bridge 122.8, west of Wilbern, and GP38 2338 does just that as it slips under the rural structure with train 113 on May 18, 1985. Shortly after this photo was taken, the bridge was torn down and replaced by a concrete structure a few yards to the right. *Below* . . . U30CG 8003 and U33C 8500 swing by milepost 123 in October 1978 with eastbound mixed freight. The six U30CG's (8000-8005) were all retired in September 1980, and the twenty-five members of the 8500 class (8500-8524) went to scrap four years later. *Right* . . . SD45 rebuild 5337 leads eastbound pigs at mile 123 in May 1985. The 5337 was painted in the red/yellow/black merger scheme a year later, one of 306 locomotives (and ten slugs) to get the treatment before painting was halted in July 1986 after the AT&SF/SP merger was denied. *Three photos: Joe McMillan.*

Certainly the most imposing structure on the east end of the Illinois Division is the Illinois River bridge at mile 128.2, just east of Chillicothe. The first bridge over the river was a single track structure built in 1887 and 1888. A swing span was added in 1906 to allow passage of river vessels. The bridge had very long approaches giving the entire structure a length of 10,164 feet, nearly two miles! The present double-track bridge was placed in service on July 15, 1931. It crosses the river at a much higher elevation than the original bridge. While the new bridge crosses the Illinois at the same general location as the old one, it crosses at a slightly different angle. To avoid interruption in train service, the new bridge was built over the top of the old structure. After the new bridge was placed in service, the old crossing was removed. The present bridge is 1695 feet long and consists of one 446-foot skewed through truss, three deck trusses and two 70-foot approach deck girders. The "traditional" spot to photograph the bridge is from the southeast quadrant. Access to the area is off Illinois Route 26 south of Lacon, Illinois, and the best photography is mid-morning. *Above* . . . On April 30, 1988, an SD45-2 leads eastbound trailers over the Illinois River. *Top* . . . Merger red GP30 2717 glides across the bridge in August 1986 with a westbound local. *Top: Dave Oroszi; above: Mike Dannemann.*

Chillicothe, Illinois, mile 130, was the headquarters of the old Illinois Division when it extended only from Chicago to Fort Madison. On September 2, 1956, the old Illinois and Missouri Divisions were consolidated and headquarters established at Fort Madison. Chillicothe has been a crew change point for many years, but there have been changes. Santa Fe enginemen have been running through between Chicago and Fort Madison since the early 1970s, but most trainmen still change at Chillicothe. However, some intermodals, such as trains 199 and 991, have assigned crews and blast through Chillicothe without a crew change. On March 3rd and 4th, 1969, when the two photos below were taken, all freight crews changed at Chillicothe. *Below* . . . FP45s 104 and 106 ease out of Chillicothe with train 55 and a long string of pigs. The FP45s were not regular power for freights at this time, but these units were working their way back to Kansas City after being used on a special work train out of Chillicothe the day before. The work extra was helping research personnel determine the cause of a passenger train derailment west of town a month earlier. *Bottom* . . . Just after dawn U30CGs 404 and 405 slow for a crew change. The U28CGs and U30CGs, originally purchased for passenger service, were then being reassigned to freight duties. These two units will soon be renumbered 8004 and 8005 and will lose their passenger paint. *Three photos: Joe McMillan.*

Top left . . . An A-B-B set of warbonnet F-units pause for a crew change in March 1969. The 43C became the 307C in April 1971 and 331L in March 1973. It was rebuilt to CF7 2444 in August 1977 and eventually wound up on the North Shore Railroad at Northumberland, Pennsylvania. *Lower left* . . . Santa Fe and Amtrak team up on May 5, 1987 to operate an Operation Lifesaver special from Chicago to Galesburg and return. Various local, state and railroad officials are aboard to promote grade crossing safety. During the OL presentation at Chillicothe, a father helps his son up to the cab of SDFP45 5998. *Above* . . . It's Independence Day 1977 as Amtrak Train No. 16, the eastbound LONE STAR, poses at Chillicothe during a regular station stop. SDP40Fs 517 and 501 head today's 10 car train. Both units are painted in the second of three paint schemes applied to SDP40Fs. The first featured a solid red nose, the second sported wide blue and red bands bordered and separated by a narrow white band, as shown, and the third had three equal red, white and blue bands, Amtrak's current scheme. The LONE STAR is long gone, but Chillicothe is still a regular stop for the SOUTHWEST CHIEF. *Four photos: Joe McMillan.*

Chillicothe Yard is used today primarily for car storage. *Top left* . . . Freshly painted U23B 6337 sets out a long string of tank cars at the west end of the yard on May 18, 1985. Sixteen years earlier . . . *bottom left* . . . a trio of GP20s pull out of Chillicothe with mixed freight for the west. Santa Fe's 75 GP20s have carried three series of road numbers. They were delivered in 1960 and 1961 as 1100s, but were renumbered to 3100s in the 1969-1970 general locomotive renumbering. They became 3000s as they emerged from remanufacturing between January 1977 and August 1981. Most of the fleet was still active in 1989, but 19 were sold to the new TP&W in February.

As mentioned in an earlier caption, Santa Fe ran a series of tests west of Chillicothe on March 3rd and 4th, 1969, in an attempt to determine the cause of a derailment to No. 23 on February 9. *Above* . . . FP45s 104 and 106 make one of many runs over instrumented track (behind the photographer) with a consist similar to that which derailed. The next day, a pair of GE U28CGs would pull the same cars. As a result of these and other tests, Santa Fe's U28CGs and U30CGs were removed from passenger service and reassigned to freight. That's No. 18, the eastbound SUPER CHIEF, disappearing in the background. *Three photos: Joe McMillan.*

The ruling grade for westbound traffic between Chicago and Kansas City is Edelstein Hill, located between miles 132 and 138, west of Chillicothe. Rails are lifted 287 feet on a grade just exceeding 1%. The double track main twists through 10 curves, the most famous of which is Houlihan's curve at mile 133 where trains bend around 60 degrees of curvature. While the hill presents an occasional operational problem for the railroad, it is a boon for photographers. Trains pass by relatively slowly and the scenery is great. *Above* . . . Local LIL031, which we viewed earlier setting out tank cars, barrels around Houlihan's curve at 5:33 p.m. with a short train behind the 6337, 3036 and 3629 (U23B/GP20/GP39-2). *Top right* . . . Conrail GP40-2 3344 and C30-7 6592 handle a westbound run-through on June 4, 1988. *Bottom right* . . . Three SDFP45s, 5998, 5993 and 5995 make the curve on October 22, 1988 with train 148, the westbound Hyundai double stack. This is the same train photographed by Steve Cigolle at Wilbern shortly before. (See page 68.) *Above: Joe McMillan; two photos right page: Mike Danneman.*

To visit Edelstein Hill by automobile, take Truitt Avenue west out of Chillicothe a few miles to a point where the road and tracks begin to separate. Make a right turn onto Santa Fe Road, then an immediate left onto the gravel road following along the south side of the tracks. Travel a few hundred yards up the road and you'll see Houlihan's curve at mile 133. Continue uphill a few miles and you'll cross over the tracks at mile 136 on a new concrete bridge, an excellent spot from which to photograph or watch trains.

Like the Wilbern area, Edelstein Hill is a good place to photograph Santa Fe trains in fall colors. *Above* . . . A pleasant day in October 1976 finds U33Cs 8516 and 8508 lifting train 123 upgrade at mile 136. The 25 members of the 8500 class would be around another nine years before going to scrap. *Top right* . . . Twelve years later, locomotive engineer Warren Scholl has a set of Rio Grande SD40T-2s in "run 8" on the point of Wheatfield coal empties returning west on the C-SRKC. It's 4:46 p.m., October 22, 1988. *Bottom right* . . . A little hiking was necessary to photograph C30-7s 8147 and 8148 as they drift downgrade past milepost 134 with train 571 on a sunny morning in October 1987. *Two photos right page: Steve Cigolle; above: Joe McMillan.*

Twenty years ago, the trackside observer could be certain that one of two locomotive types would be seen leading Santa Fe freight trains between Chicago and Fort Madison: an 1100 class GP20 or a 1600 class U25B. Automatic Train Control (ATC), more commonly known as cab signals, was in use between East Fort Madison (now Niota), mile 230.9, and Pequot, mile 57.2. The only freight units equipped with cab signals at the time were 1100s and 1600s. Signal indications were displayed inside the locomotive cab on a special device resembling the familiar highway stop light. The Interstate Commerce Commission ordered Santa Fe to install the cab signal system, which was placed in service in two phases. The first phase, between Chillicothe and East Fort Madison was completed in January 1925, and the second phase, between Chillicothe and Pequot was completed in March 1928. The ICC order was rescinded in 1928 and no further installations were made on the Santa Fe. The system was removed from service in several phases and was gone by October 1970, allowing locomotives of any class to lead trains. *Top left* . . . While one of Santa Fe's Indian steel gangs lay three-rail "Lionel" track, three GP20s, an Alco RSD-15 and a GP35 haul a long string of box cars up Edelstein on August 28, 1969. A month earlier . . . *bottom left* . . . GP20 1161 passes milepost 136 with westbound pigs. *Above* . . . Of course, Santa Fe's passenger locomotive fleet was also equipped with cab signals. In August 1969, train No. 1, the SAN FRANCISCO CHIEF, speeds west behind an A-A-B-B-A warbonnet combination. It was common for passenger consists to have two forward-facing cab units. Should the first cab become disabled for any reason, the train could proceed with minimum delay. *Three photos: Joe McMillan.*

Above . . . The green of spring is starting to show at mile 136 as GP30 2723 and a variety of small units struggle uphill with a mainline local. It's May Day, 1988. *Top right* . . . On October 2, 1976, U25Bs 6602, 6606 and GP20 3158 approach mile 136 with train 372, an eastbound Conrail run-through enroute to Streator. *Bottom right* . . . Second 18, the eastbound SUPER CHIEF, crosses over at Edelstein (mile 138) in August 1969 to avoid the steel gang working on the south track. Today, this set of crossovers is protected by a pair of signal bridges, not necessary in 1969 when the cab signal system was in place. *Above: Mike Danneman; two photos right page: Joe McMillan.*

Between Edelstein and Williamsfield (mile 158.3), the undulating main line skirts more corn fields. At mile 139.2, just west of Edelstein, Chicago & North Western's St. Louis line dips under the Santa Fe, and at Princeville (mile 144.7), Rock Island's Peoria-Colona line once crossed at grade. Monica (mile 148.3) once boasted a depot and a tower (protecting a long-abandoned crossing at grade with a CB&Q branch connecting Buda and Elmwood, Illinois.) Effective May 21, 1989, Princeville and Monica are no longer considered "stations" on the Santa Fe and their names have been stricken from the timetable. *Bottom right* . . . You're aboard F7A 44C on the eastbound SAN FRANCISCO CHIEF slamming through Williamsfield on April 25, 1969. The station was being closed at the time and was removed shortly thereafter. At Williamsfield, the main line begins the gentle descent to the Spoon River at Dahinda (mile 163.3). *Top right* . . . Train 571 bangs across the Spoon at 10:15 a.m., September 10, 1988, behind the 8047, 3817 and 5022 (C30-7/GP50/SD40-2). *Above* . . . Brand new GE Dash 8-40B 7437 heels into the curve at mile 164 west of Dahinda with the eastbound mail train, Q-LANY, one of six eastbound trains by this point in an hour! It's 2:33 p.m., May 21, 1989. *Top right: Steve Cigolle; above and bottom right: Joe McMillan.*

Galesburg, Illinois (mile 177.5) is the county seat of Knox County and home of poet Carl Sandburg. In railroad circles, Galesburg is probably better known for its large Burlington Northern yard and facilities than for the Santa Fe. The AT&SF, however, considers Galesburg an important station and recently completed a new piggyback facility there. Galesburg received a new station in 1964, replacing a large, fortress-like structure. *Above . . .* In the early evening of October 2, 1972, Amtrak's SUPER CHIEF makes a station stop at Galesburg. *Below . . .* Santa Fe's eastbound SAN FRANCISCO CHIEF slows for a station stop in April 1969. *Above: Robert P. Schmidt; below: Joe McMillan.*

Above . . . TV news cameramen photograph SDFP45 5998 and Amtrak F40PH 381 on the point of an Operation Livesaver special at Galesburg, May 5, 1987. The seven-car train waits at Galesburg after turning on the wye west of the depot. In a few minutes, the special will leave for Chicago, its riders having spent the day spreading the gospel on grade crossing safety. *Below* . . . Second 18, the eastbound EL CAPITAN, pauses at Galesburg on July 1, 1969. Six F-unit warbonnets are up front today. The lead unit, F3A 31C, later became CF7 2636. It now hauls freight cars for the Washington Central Railroad out of Yakima, Washington, as its 402. *Two photos: Joe McMillan.*

Bottom left . . . Santa Fe's double track main line crosses over Burlington Northern's Chicago to Denver main just west of Cameron at mile 186.4, nine miles west of Galesburg. At 9:20 a.m., August 30, 1986, GP20 3017, GP39-2 3155 and GP35 2887 zip over the BN with an eastbound. *Top left* . . . A pair of U30CGs led by the 8000 speed west at mile 198 near Ponemah. This is straight track country. There are no curves and little scenery from mile 184.6 east of Cameron to mile 204 near Media, a distance of 19.4 miles. *Above* . . . It's April 7, 1969 and the end is near for the Media depot. Several Illinois Division stations were being closed and torn down during this period. *Below* . . . Certainly the most imposing structure in the area is the 737-foot Media trestle at mile 203.6. The trestle is supported by seven steel towers and crosses the Ellison Creek valley. On the last day of May 1986, merger red C30-7 8077 and three mates head eastbound pigs across the bridge. *Top left: Jim Primm; bottom left: Dave Oroszi; two photos right page: Joe McMillan.*

Vegetation was sparse around Media trestle twenty years ago making the bridge easier to photograph. *Below and top left . . .* Second 18 speeds across the bridge on July 1, 1969. F3A 26C leads the five-unit consist. *Bottom left . . .* Several months earlier, the westbound SAN FRANCISCO CHIEF crosses behind F7A 339. *Three photos: Joe McMillan.*

The best photography today is of eastbound trains from the south side of the bridge in mid-morning light. Westbound trains can be photographed in late afternoon from the north side. Visitors have easy access to the bridge from a paved rural road running along the south side of the railroad and intersecting State Route 116 at an underpass on the outskirts of Media.

Stronghurst (mile 208.9) is 4.5 miles west of Media on another long stretch of straight track: 11 miles (mile 204 to 215). It was an important livestock shipping point in the 1940s. Though long closed, the depot still stands in late-1989. *Above . . .* Red GP30 2717 leads train 301 through town at 11:32 a.m., May 31, 1986. *Below . . .* Train 113 speeds west at mile 213.7, just out of Decorra, Illinois, on August 31, 1986 behind the 8150, 5256, 2887, 3155 and 3017 (C30-7/SDF40-2/GP35/GP39-2/GP20). *"Axy Dent" sign on Stronghurst depot and above: Joe McMillan; below: Dave Oroszi.*

Above . . . The day before, another train 113 passes the station sign at Lomax, mile 218.9. Lomax is Santa Fe's connection with the TP&W Railway Corporation. TP&W trains have trackage rights over the Santa Fe from here to Fort Madison. Until the 1960s, Lomax was also served by the CB&Q. The Burlington line came up from Quincy to Dallas City, ran along the south side of the Santa Fe to Lomax, curved under the AT&SF at mile 217.8 and ran north to Burlington, Iowa. At one time, this Burlington line provided TP&W with its western connection. The Peoria Road joined the CB&Q at Iowa Junction, the point where the Burlington track passed under the Santa Fe. This connection was severed in 1927, and on August 6th of that year interchange was established with the Santa Fe. *Below* . . . The Dallas City depot (mile 224.8), built in 1888, was still open when photographed on April 24, 1969. The structure was retired on February 9, 1971 and removed shortly thereafter. *Above: Dave Oroszi; below: Joe McMillan.*

Santa Fe's main line bisects Oak Street in downtown Dallas City in a narrow passage between main street buildings. The crossing is not usually blocked for long, however, as trains may pass through town at a maximum speed of 70 m.p.h. *Above* . . . It's 9:15 a.m. on a quiet Sunday morning in May 1988 and we're looking west as GP20 3014 zips across Oak Street with a work train for the Peoria Subdivision. Note the Mississippi River in the background beyond the locomotive. *Top left* . . . Merger red B23-7 6374 (later renumbered 7208, then back to 6374) slips through town at 5:59 p.m., May 31, 1986, with Peoria Subdivision train 352. The eastbounder will leave the main line at Lomax and travel to Peoria over the former TP&W. This wide angle view looks east up Oak Street past the Anguish & Wolfenbarger Ford Company and Pioneer Lumber, the latter an important shipper in the 1940s. *Bottom left* . . . SF30B 7200, the one and only such unit on the roster, passes the Dallas City station sign with eastbound trailers on April 24, 1988. The 7200 was the prototype for a proposed remanufacturing program for 6300-6348 series U23Bs. Even though the prototype was successful, it was decided to sell the remaining members of the class instead of rebuilding them. Cleburne shops in Texas built the 7200 from the 6332 in July 1987. *Top left and above: Joe McMillan; bottom left Mike Danneman.*

On October 23, 1886, the Mississippi River Railroad and Toll Bridge Company was incorporated in Illinois to build and operate Santa Fe's first bridge across the Mississippi. The first train — a work train behind 4-4-0 539 — crossed the structure on December 1, 1887. The bridge featured a single track railroad with a single lane roadway on either side of the track. The crossing was 2963 feet long and consisted of eight through truss spans (one was a swing section) resting on stone piers. The present bridge, 3347 feet in length, was built upstream from the old structure and crossed the river at a slightly different angle to avoid ninety degree approach curves. (The east approach today is 59 degrees, the west 65 degrees.) On July 25, 1927, 2-8-2 3268 hauled the first train across the new bridge. The most notable feature of the structure is its huge 525-foot swing span, the longest and heaviest in the country when constructed. A two-lane toll road is carried on the upper deck of the truss spans above the double track main line. The bridge also carries trains over the state line into Iowa (at mile 231.8).

Top left . . . On the Fourth of July, 1969, Second 18, the EL CAPITAN, eases off the Illinois end of the Mississippi River bridge behind a pair of 100 class FP45s. Four months earlier, on the opposite end of the structure. . . *bottom left* . . . the SUPER C curves off the bridge as it approaches Fort Madison and a crew change. *Above* . . . Filmed from the roadway deck above the tracks on October 22, 1981, GP38 3503 (since renumbered 2303) and mates guide eastbound pigs onto the bridge at 30 m.p.h. The big building in the background is the home of Sheaffer pens. *Two photos left page: Joe McMillan; above: Jim Primm*

Above . . . The TP&W (both new and old) had trackage rights over the Santa Fe between Lomax and Fort Madison, a distance of 16 miles. On a beautiful morning in March 1969, TP&W train 122 crawls onto the bridge with freight for East Peoria. With the January 1, 1984 merger of the "old" TP&W into the Santa Fe, the 700 became AT&SF 3285, then 2785. The GP30 remains active in 1989. *Top right* . . . Five months later, GP20 1168 leads a pair of GP35s and a GP30 off the swing span with a westbound. The 1961-built 1168 later became the 3168, then 3068. It was sold to the "new" TP&W in February 1989, one of 19 GP20s included in the sale. *Bottom right* . . . Train 23, the former GRAND CANYON, passes by displayed 4-8-4 2913 at Fort Madison's Riverview Park on March 2, 1969. The big steamer was donated to the city in September 1959. *Three photos: Joe McMillan.*

Fort Madison, the "Gem City," was named after an old fort and trading post established in 1805 by Lt. Zebulon M. Pike, for whom Pike's Peak was later named. Though its importance has diminished in recent years, Fort Madison has always been a major Santa Fe location. A locomotive and car shop was established there, and by 1910, 500 people were employed. For many years, Fort Madison was the division point between the old Illinois and Missouri Divisions. In September 1956, the two divisions were consolidated into the "new" Illinois Division with headquarters at Fort Madison. For most of its rail history, two timetable stations were located at Fort Madison. The brick passenger depot downtown, completed in 1910, was designated Fort Madison, mile 232.9. The yards, shops and other facilities were at Shopton, mile 234.6. Two towers controlled the entrances to Shopton Yard. Tower A was located at mile 234.1 and Tower B at mile 235.9. Both were gone by the mid-1950s after the coming of Centralized Traffic Control (CTC) rendered them obsolete. In 1968, the company completed a new passenger station at Shopton and it became the Fort Madison station (mile 234.3). The old depot downtown was abandoned and sold. The Shopton name was dropped from the timetable on June 8, 1969.

Top left . . . The old Fort Madison station is pictured in April 1969, just after it closed. The building has changed little externally since its completion in 1910. It is now a museum, complete with displayed Santa Fe caboose 999235. The building in the right background is the CB&Q station, now Burlington Northern, which is Fort Madison's other railroad. *Bottom left* . . . First and Second 18, the SUPER CHIEF and EL CAPITAN line up at the fueling facility at Fort Madison on August 21, 1969. The 25C was traded in to EMD a year later on a new GP38. *Above* . . . Amtrak No. 16, the TEXAS CHIEF, pulls into Fort Madison's "new" station on May 4, 1974. In fifteen days the train will be renamed LONE STAR. *Below* . . . On April 28, 1969, FP45 100 leads No. 18, the combined SUPER CHIEF/EL CAPITAN, out of Fort Madison near the site of long-abandoned Tower A. *Four photos: Joe McMillan.*

Before continuing west, let's journey across Santa Fe's Peoria Subdivision, the former Toledo, Peoria and Western Railroad. The TP&W is an old railroad with a colorful and interesting history. The Peoria Road was largely in place and operating before the first Santa Fe rail was laid. By 1868, the TP&W was operating from the Indiana-Illinois state line on the east through Peoria, La Harpe to Keokuk, Iowa on the west. On November 27, 1871, the TP&W opened a line from La Harpe northwest to Burlington, Iowa. When the Santa Fe built through sixteen years later, it crossed over this line at mile 217.8 near the present station of Lomax. The Lomax to Burlington segment became part of a CB&Q line from Quincy to Burlington, and the La Harpe to Lomax portion became TP&W's connection to the Santa Fe. In February 1960, the Santa Fe and Pennsylvania Railroad each acquired a 50% share of the TP&W. In July 1979, Santa Fe purchased Pennsylvania's (by then Penn Central) 50% equity interest in the TP&W. The ICC approved Santa Fe's control of TP&W effective March 1, 1981. With the formation of Conrail on April 1, 1976, the TP&W was forced to acquire the ex-Pennsylvania line from Logansport, Indiana to the Illinois state line at Effner, TP&W's easternmost point. This segment was not included in the Conrail system and the Peoria Road had to acquire it to preserve its eastern connection. On January 1, 1984, the TP&W was merged into the Santa Fe, becoming the Peoria District—Peoria Subdivision after October 27, 1985—of the Illinois Division. With the merger came sixteen TP&W locomotives, three cabooses, a number of freight cars and 311.6 route miles of trackage (Logansport to Lomax, 283.2 miles and La Harpe to Keokuk, 28.4 miles). When additional business on the Peoria line (primarily intermodal traffic at the Hoosier Lift terminal near Remington, Indiana) did not materialize, the line was offered for sale. After several false starts, the Peoria Subdivision was sold on February 3, 1989 to the TP&W Acquisition Corporation, which operates the line as the Toledo, Peoria and Western Railroad Corporation.

Even though it's Sunday, Santa Fe's Vegetation Control Department is busy. This train will spend several days on the Peoria Subdivision applying weed killer chemicals to the right of way. Spray car 199207, built from a former Santa Fe baggage car, is the workhorse of the train. *Above* . . . The spray train turns on the wye at La Harpe, mile 195.5, and a few minutes later . . . *right* . . . weed chemicals and other supplies are loaded aboard. After loading, GP20 3014, coupled to the rear of the train, will drag the cars 11 miles west to Lomax where spraying will begin. B*elow* . . . The work train sprays eastward at mile 173.5, just west of Bushnell, where the train will tie up for the night. The date is May 22, 1988. *Three photos: Joe McMillan.*

Above . . . The work train sprays through Good Hope, Illinois, mile 179.6. The crew disperses chemicals carefully through towns and sensitive areas to avoid damage to flowers, crops and other desired vegetation.

The 28.4 mile La Harpe-Keokuk route was TP&W's original west end main line, a status held until the La Harpe-Lomax segment gained prominence in later times. The line angled southwest from La Harpe to Elvaston, Illinois (mile 216) where an old Wabash branch from Bluffs—75.8 miles southeast—joined and shared the TP&W route to Hamilton. The Wabash branch later became Norfolk & Western, but N&W trains stopped running to Keokuk in December 1978, long before Santa Fe came on the scene. The five-mile Warsaw branch leaves the main at Hamilton (mile 222.6), on the east side of the Mississippi. The branch hasn't been used in years, but it once served a coal dock on the river. The main line crossed the Mississippi on a double deck rail-highway bridge owned by the Keokuk and Hamilton Bridge Company, and later by the city of Keokuk. Freight was interchanged with CB&Q's Burlington-St. Louis line (later BN) and Rock Island's Eldon-Keokuk branch. The Rock Island branch was later abandoned, but its Keokuk trackage became the Keokuk Junction Railway in 1981. The TP&W operated out of a small yard on the waterfront and usually kept two locomotives there. The Santa Fe acquired the La Harpe-Keokuk branch with the January 1, 1984 merger and operated it as the La Harpe Industrial Spur until it was sold to the Keokuk Junction Railway on December 24, 1986. *Top right* . . . GP30 2783 and GP20 3003 ease out of Keokuk on the approach to the Mississippi River bridge. *Later*. . . the pair cross a rural road at mile 196 on the outskirts of La Harpe. The date is July 16, 1986. *Above: Joe McMillan; two photos right: Michael W. Blaszak.*

Above . . . Enroute to East Peoria, Santa Fe train 352 crosses over Illinois Route 9 just east of La Harpe. It's 5:50 p.m., August 31, 1986. Up front today are the 3612, 3032 and 2748 (GP39-2/GP20/GP30). *Below* . . . B23-7 6356 leads a westbound Cilco coal train across the Illinois River at Peoria on July 16, 1986. Moving alongside the Santa Fe train is Peoria & Pekin Union switcher 607 with a string of cars for Peoria. The vertical lift P&PU bridge is new; it was built in 1983 and 1984 to replace a bascule structure. *Above: Dave Oroszi; below: Michael W. Blaszak.*

For years, the TP&W operated a local between East Peoria and an industrial area at Kolbe (Mapleton), a distance of 14 miles. The Kolbe local continued to run after the merger, often in charge of a pair of Santa Fe GP7s. Three TP&W bay window cabooses came with the merger. One was retired immediately and placed in a city park in Oklahoma. The other two were painted bright Santa Fe red, yellow and black, classed as Ce-13s and numbered 999653 and 999654. The cars were assigned to East Peoria where they saw frequent service on the Kolbe local. *Above* . . . Geeps 2005 and 2004 pass by freshly painted 999654 while switching in Peoria on May 12, 1984, five months after the merger. Later in the day, the conductor walks to the Kolbe station . . . *below* . . . for his switch list. The local will spend several hours switching industries here before returning to East Peoria. Caboose 999654 was sold in October 1987 for display at Chatsworth, Illinois while the 999653 went to a scrapper in Clovis, New Mexico in 1988. Geep 2004 is still on the roster, but the 2005 was retired in August 1988 and sold. *Two photos: Joe McMillan.*

East Peoria was the headquarters for the "old" TP&W, and it is the operating headquarters for the "new" TP&W. During the five years and 33 days the railroad was a Santa Fe branch, however, Fort Madison call the shots. East Peoria remained a crew change point and several operating officials were stationed there, but it lost much of its former prominence. The Santa Fe tore down the roundhouse and several other buildings during its tenure, and made many other changes. When these photos were taken on February 20, 1984, 51 days after the merger, the railroad still had a TP&W look to it. Much of the Peoria Road's locomotive fleet had been sold off prior to the merger, but the engines that were kept continued to called East Peoria home for a few months following the merger, although they carried Santa Fe numbers. *Top right* . . . The 3565, 6369 and 3562 zip along with westbound train 1172 (Logansport to East Peoria, formerly TP&W No. 21) between Secor and Eureka. That's US 24 paralleling the rails. Later . . . *above* . . . the same locomotive consist reflects late afternoon sun at East Peoria. Earlier in the day . . . *bottom right* . . . the 3567, 3549 and 3566 idle at East Peoria awaiting their next call to duty. TP&W's 11 GP38-2's, built in 1977 and 1978, carried numbers 2001-2011. They became 3561-3571 after the merger, but were renumbered again in 1985 to 2370-2380. All 11 units were painted in Santa Fe blue and yellow shortly after the merger, but by July 1986 units 2370-2375 had been repainted merger red and yellow. About half the class is presently assigned to yard and transfer duties at Kansas City, while the rest are scattered across the railroad, usually working secondary assignments. *Three photos: Joe McMillan.*

Like the Pekin District, the Peoria Road was subject to heavy drifting from winter snows. In February 1985, a storm paralyzed the TP&W, particularly the east end. Santa Fe rotary plow 199361 was again called to duty and spent three days clearing the line. Plowing began the third day at Forrest and slowly proceeded east. The deepest drifts were between Forrest and Chatsworth. *Above* . . . The rotary nearly chokes on a big mouthful at mile 43. *Top left* . . . After clearing the worst drifts, the work train moves into Chatsworth, mile 40.3, where it pauses briefly before continuing. Later in the day . . . *bottom left* . . . the plow bounces across the Missouri Pacific (formerly C&EI) at Watseka, Illinois, mile 11.1. The date is February 15, 1985. *Three photos: Joe McMillan.*

Top right . . . Just after sunup, rotary 199361 moves through two-foot snow on the outskirts of Forrest. The Interstate 57 overpass (mile 25.3) just west of Gilman . . . *above* . . . provides an interesting perspective as the plow breaks through a small drift. Locomotives 3025, 3036 and 6385 (GP20/GP20/B23-7) are the force behind the plow. The 3025 is wired directly to the rotary and provides power to operate the blade while the other two units furnish traction. Three days before, on February 12 . . . *bottom right* . . . GP39-2 3675 leads an eastbound toward El Paso, fighting deep drifts all the way. Conditions are too severe to continue, so the crew will leave their train at El Paso and return to East Peoria with the engines. *Bottom right: Roger A. Holmes; above and top right: Joe McMillan.*

Top left . . . B23-7 6410 and mates kick up dust as they speed westbound freight through El Paso on May 27, 1988. The three other photos are deceiving because they appear to be Santa Fe trains, but they aren't! *Above* . . . The wind chill factor exceeds fifty below on a bitterly cold December 23, 1983 as a pair of GP38s led by the 3500 hold the siding at Cruger (mile 94) with TP&W's Effner Local, train 1173, as a westbound coal train passes. The "old" TP&W is about to see its last Christmas; this will be Santa Fe's Peoria District in nine days. Just over five years later, on February 3, 1989, Santa Fe sold the railroad to the TP&W Acquisition Corporation. Included in the sale were 19 Santa Fe GP20s. *Below* . . . A "new" TP&W eastbound rattles across the IC diamond at Gilman, Illinois on February 20, 1989. GP20 3073, leading the train, is one of five merger red GP20s included in the sale. Later . . . *bottom left* . . . the same train passes through Kentland, Indiana. *Top left: Mark Danneman; above: Joe McMillan; bottom left and below: Melvern Finzer.*

On January 17, 1968, Santa Fe inaugurated the Super C, a high speed, premium service Chicago to Los Angeles piggybacker. The train was greeted with less than enthusiastic response from shippers. It slowly gained some traffic, but not enough to justify its existence. In April 1969, the U. S. Postal Service came to the rescue in form of a contract to handle parcel post between Chicago and Los Angeles. *Above . . .* On April 17, 1969, U30CGs 404, 405 and U28CG 356 slow for a crew change at Fort Madison with the first westbound Super C mail train. *Below . . .* Four months later, No. 23 accelerates out of Fort Madison behind FP45 104 and U30CG 403. It was rare to see an FP45 on this train; it was rarer still to see an FP45 and a U30CG coupled in the same consist. FP45 104, later 5944, was destroyed in an accident in Texas in September 1981. In 1989 it was the only EMD cowl unit off the roster. *Both photos: Joe McMillan.*

Above . . . It's early morning, May 2, 1976, as an eastbound director's special is serviced at Fort Madison. FP45 5942 and a pair of SD45s do the honors. The 5942 has changed considerably since this photograph. The 3600 h.p. unit was remanufactured in November 1982, emerging from San Bernardino shops as SDFP45 5992. In April 1986, it was painted merger red in anticipation of the AT&SF-SP consolidation. It was renumbered 101 and painted warbonnet red and silver in June 1989, heralding Santa Fe's new "Super Fleet." *Below* . . . It's May Day 1969 as U25Bs 1602, 1612, 1609 and 1614 ease westbound freight out of Fort Madison. The company's sixteen 1600s became 6600s a year later and were gone by spring 1979. Note the old locomotive shop buildings in the distant left and the Mississippi River at right. *Above: Jim Primm; below: Joe McMillan.*

Top left . . . U28CG 358 eases train 99, the westbound Super C, by a mishap on the south main at the west end of Fort Madison yard in May 1969.

Santa Fe has only 20.2 route miles of main line trackage in Iowa, but there are two nice photo locations. The first is at the old station location of New Boston, mile 244, 9.7 miles west of Fort Madison. U. S. Route 218 passes over the tracks at this point giving the visitor a nice view of westbound trains. *Bottom left* . . . GP20 1118 leads a pair of GP35s and a string of boxcars at New Boston on September 27, 1969. Seventeen years later . . . *above* . . . GP35 2851 pilots more boxcars west as it leads train 253 (from Peoria) toward Kansas City. During the interval between the two photos, welded rail has replaced jointed and the vegetation has proliferated. *Three photos: Joe McMillan.*

The second Iowa photo location is at the Argyle crossovers at mile 246.3, 1.6 miles east of the small village of Argyle. A rural bridge spans the main line at this location. To visit the spot, you must follow a gravel road out of town that eventually winds up here. It is a nice spot to spend the day. *Above* . . . On September 11, 1969, No. 1, the SAN FRANCISCO CHIEF, crosses over from the south to the north main at Argyle behind F7A 44C. *Right page* . . . Years later, on May 16, 1987, two Conrail run-throughs meet at Argyle shortly after sunrise. *Three photos: Joe McMillan.*

Above . . . A 900-foot deck truss at mile 252 carries the main line across the Des Moines River and into Missouri. At 2:17 p.m., September 5, 1988, B36-7 7491 and three mates slip across the structure with eastbound train 881. Rock Island's long-abandoned Eldon-Keokuk branch passed under the Santa Fe at mile 251.8, just out of the photo at right. The old station of Dumas was located just off the Missouri end of the bridge at mile 252.3. Watering facilities and a depot were located there, as well as tracks to an old stone quarry. *Left* . . . Revere, mile 256, was the first station in Missouri (after Dumas' demise) until May 21, 1989, when its name was deleted from the timetable. Back on October 21, 1969, however, Revere was still a "station" on Illinois Division's Third District when GP20 1103 led westbound boxcars through the tiny village. The concrete overpass in the background is Clark Country Route C; the photo was taken from bridge 256.6. *Above: Steve Cigolle; left: Joe McMillan.*

Most of northeast Missouri is heavily wooded, and consequently, access to the tracks is limited. Roads in the area do not parallel the main line, however, the country abounds in rural overpasses, many of which provide excellent vantage points from which to view or photograph trains. *Above* . . . SDF40-2 5256—formerly Amtrak SDP40F 640—leans into a curve at mile 260 as it approaches the State Highway 81 overpass east of Medill with Chicago-bound pigs. At Medill, mile 263.1, the main line passes under U. S. Highway 136, and at one time crossed CB&Q's old Alexandria (near Keokuk) to Clarinda, Iowa branch. The CB&Q and Santa Fe shared a brick station at Medill and a tower guarded the crossing. The station was closed in November 1957 and today only a station sign marks the spot. On New Year's Eve 1887, officials drove home the last spike completing the Kansas City-Chicago line at a point just west of Medill. Near that spot . . . *top left* . . . three TP&W units speed a westbound run-through around the curve at mile 266.7 on October 9, 1980. For a short time, TP&W locomotives ran through between East Peoria and Kansas City. *Bottom left* . . . The next day, looking the opposite direction from bridge 266.7, Amtrak No. 4 meets a westbound Conrail run-through. *Right* . . . Eight years later, SD45 rebuild 5376—formerly 5624—rounds the same curve with pigs for the west. *Four photos: Jim Primm.*

Wyaconda, Missouri, mile 272.3, once boasted a track side depot, stock yard and water tank. While the small town still exists, its name was stricken from the timetable with the purge of May 21, 1989. However, twenty years prior, on September 24, 1969 . . . *above* . . . Wyaconda was still an active station when train 99, the westbound SUPER C, slammed across the wig-wag-protected crossing a few feet east of the depot. Powering the hotshot this day is U28CG 357 and a pair of 8500 class U33Cs. *Below* . . . Mr. Merlin Armstrong was agent at Wyaconda when this photo was taken on May 27, 1969. Mr. Armstrong, owner of the tri-color Dodge, was also the mayor of Wyaconda. The company filed to abandon the station in March 1972. It was closed shortly thereafter and moved to a nearby location . *Two photos: Joe McMillan.*

An overpass just east of Wyaconda (bridge 270.9) provides a nice vantage point for viewing trains. *Above* . . . A TP&W run-through behind GP38-2 2006—now Santa Fe 2375— speeds mixed freight west on October 8, 1980. *Below* . . . Santa Fe's only SF30B (rebuilt from a GE U23B) leads a string of pigs toward Kansas City at the same spot on October 5, 1988. *Two photos: Jim Primm.*

The small town of Rutledge lies 11 rail miles west of Wyaconda. The overpass just north of town at mile 282.1 carries Scotland County Road A over the tracks and provides the visitor with an excellent view of westbound trains. If you had been there on October 9, 1980 . . . *above* . . . you would have seen brand new SD40-2 5150 hurrying westbound pigs around the reverse curve. The train is climbing a 0.8% grade out of the North Fabius River valley. Although the vegetation at right has thickened somewhat during the last decade, it is still a fine place to spend an afternoon.

Two miles further west, a gravel road passes over the main line on bridge 283.9. The rails bend through 39 degrees of curvature at this point. The bridge is one of the few nice spots in the area from which to photograph eastbound trains. *Bottom right* . . . GP39-2 3449, the last unit remanufactured at Cleburne shops before the facility closed, wheels an eastbound on a beautiful morning in May 1988. *Top right* . . . Just after sunrise on June 30, 1984, SD45 rebuild 5340 reflects the early rays as it approaches the same bridge with a westbound. *Three photos: Jim Primm.*

Baring, Missouri is located at mile 290.7. Although its small depot was closed in November 1971, it still stands in 1989 and is used by maintenance of way personnel. At one time, Baring boasted a main line coal chute, water tank, water cranes, a stock yard and even a small enginehouse. All that is gone today, but the area is still interesting. Although the roadway is narrow, the State Route 15 overpass just west (geographically south) of town, mile 291.5, provides a good photo vantage point. *Top left* . . . It's 3:11 p.m. on a very hot May 16, 1987 as GP38 2310 guides train 253 (East Peoria-Kansas City) over undulating track through Baring. Note the Caterpillar tractors behind the head two cars; a dead giveaway to the train's origin.

The best photography in the area, however, is probably early morning telephoto views of eastbound trains from bridge 294.3, 3.6 rail miles west of Baring. This structure carries Knox County Road P over the tracks. Eastbound trains are viewed rounding 30 degrees of curvature beneath a pair of signal bridges. *Bottom left* . . . Not long after sunrise on October 9, 1980, C30-7 8068 rounds the curve with a consist of mixed freight. On July 1, 1984 . . . *above* . . . F45 5981 tackles the same curve. *Top left Joe McMillan; bottom left and above: Jim Primm.*

From Baring, the tracks continue southwest passing through Hurdland (mile 300.1) and Gibbs (mile 306.4). The old Quincy, Omaha & Kansas City (CB&Q) passed over the Santa Fe at Hurdland, but the crossing was abandoned in the early 1980s. Both locations had depots and stock yards at one time, but neither location appears in today's timetable. La Plata, Missouri, mile 312.7, 21.9 miles west of Baring is next. Its interesting depot still stands, and while not a manned facility, Amtrak's SOUTHWEST CHIEF still stops there daily, primarily to serve nearby Kirksville. *Above* . . . A pair of TP&W GP38-2s spliced by a Conrail motor zip through town on October 7, 1980 with freight for East Peoria. Norfolk Southern's Moberly to Des Moines line (ex-N&W, Wabash) crosses over the Santa Fe just east of the station. That vantage point. . .*below*. . . was used the same day to photograph a local heading in the east pass behind GP20 3152. *Both photos: Jim Primm.*

Above . . . A spring snow melts in the warm rays of a March 1969 sun as No. 1, the SAN FRANCISCO CHIEF, slows for a station stop behind F3A 27. *Below* . . . From the Adair County Road E overpass at mile 309.4, east of La Plata, the long lens catches Caterpillar-engined 5855 with train 321. It's 5:34 p.m., May 21 1988. *Both photos: Joe McMillan.*

ETHEL	MO	1
ETHEL	ARK	516
ETHEL	MISS	681
ETHEL	W VA	709
ETHEL	LA	926
ETHEL	WASH	1989

Elmer and Ethel lie west of La Plata at miles 322.9 and 329.7, respectively. Elmer lost its identity in May 1989 with a number of other stations, but Ethel remains a significant location, both for the railroad and the photographer. A pair of crossovers and a CTC siding are located there, as well as a portion of the old station, now classified as a "tool house." *Above*... An unusual power combination, U23C 7512 and F45 5916, speed eastbound freight through town on October 11, 1980. The U23Cs were generally found west of Kansas City in Kansas, Colorado and New Mexico. They were acquired during the summer of 1969 and were gone by early 1985.

Four rural roads pass over the tracks west of Ethel and they offer the photographer some great opportunities. The best vantage point is probably bridge 331.2, just out of town near the west crossover and siding switch. *Top right*... It's May 27, 1969 and the westbound SUPER C is highballing west behind U30CGs 401, 404 and 403. Eleven years later... *below right*... a westbound Conrail run-through meets a Santa Fe at the same spot. Note the increase in vegetation during the decade. *Above, bottom right, station signs: Jim Primm; top right: Joe McMillan; Ethel distance sign: Bryan Moseley.*

To get to bridge 331.2, drive west of Ethel on State Route 149. After a short distance, turn left on a gravel road and follow it south, bearing left at the fork. The bridge provides a nice view of trains approaching on curved track from either direction. It's productive to spend an entire day here! *Right* . . . TP&W 2008 heads a westbound run-through on a beautiful fall day in 1980. *Jim Primm.*

Above . . . Eastbound train 352 (Kansas City-East Peoria) behind merger red GP30 2770 illustrates the opposite view from bridge 331.2. It's 10:42 a.m., May 21, 1988. The rock piled along the left side of the tracks is residue from a recent ballast cleaning project. A huge machine removes the ballast, sifts out small rocks and fines, discards the fouled material and re-deposits proper-sized stones. New ballast is added and the track is lined and tamped. Clean ballast allows the track structure to drain properly preserving alignment and cross level.

If you were to take the right fork on that gravel road (refer to the photo caption on page 140), you would wind your way to bridge 332.6, the second of four rural overpasses west of Ethel. *Bottom right* . . . SD45 rebuild 5334 approaches bridge 332.6 on June 4, 1988 with a string of pigs for the west. *Top right* . . . It's about 2:45 p.m., July 12, 1989, as the first two "Super Fleet" motors, SDFP45s 102 and 101 (ex-5998 and 5992, respectively) approach the bridge with train 168. On the rear of the 51 car intermodal are four business cars of railroad officials and shippers enroute to Kansas City and Santa Fe, New Mexico. This is the first of a series of "shipper appreciation" specials behind the colorful locomotives. In July 1989, Santa Fe announced that it would be acquiring 100 new locomotives in 1990; forty EMD GP60Ms and sixty GE B40-8s, all equipped with the new "comfort" or "wide cab" pioneered by Canadian National. All 100 Super Fleet units are to be painted warbonnet red and silver, and assigned exclusively to Santa Fe's hottest intermodal trains. Santa Fe's president, Michael R. Haverty, stated in *Santa Fe Railway News* that, "While our warbonnet paint scheme is a glimpse of an honored past, it is a return to the past only in the essence of a label for speed and quality of service." To get a head start promoting speed and quality of service, the company designated the eight 5990 class SDFP45s as Super Fleet locomotives and plans to return them to their original number series and paint. San Bernardino shops released these first two in early July 1989, followed by the 100 (ex-5990) in August. *Above: Joe McMillan; top right: Bryan Moseley; bottom right: Jim Primm.*

Macon County Road VV crosses the main line at mile 334.3, the third rural overpass west of Ethel. As the case with most of the bridges in the area, the best photography here is of westbound trains in the late morning or afternoon. *Top left* . . . U25B 6606 and a pair of EMD hoods handle a westbound of mixed freight on July 6, 1977. *Bottom left* . . . Two days prior, U30CG 8004 leads another westbound at the same spot. Santa Fe was experiencing a severe motive power shortage at the time and was leasing a number of Chicago & North Western and Canadian National locomotives. The second unit is a C&NW GP30. Note the "high and wide" cars on the head end. Vegetation on the distant hill has increased dramatically since these photographs were taken. *Above* . . . Brand new SD40-2s 5201, 5200 and 5206, shown making their first revenue run, lead westbound freight by mile 336, the location of the former station of Hart, Missouri. The train is about to cross Macon County Road Z; a crew change at Marceline is 11.3 miles away. A depot and stock pen were once located here, but there is no trace of them today. *Below* . . . The fourth rural overpass in the area is bridge 336.9, which carries a little used dirt road over the tracks. Access to the overpass is generally difficult during wet weather, but that was not the worry on Independence Day 1977 as U25B 6606 speeds east with an intermodal train. Trailing the GE is a trio of leased CN motors. *Four photos: Jim Primm.*

Marceline, Missouri, mile 347.3, is the boyhood home of Walt Disney, as the sign over the office door proclaims. Until September 1956, the classy brick station, opened on April 10th, 1913, was headquarters for the Missouri Division. Marceline was a major railroad location, featuring a large coaling tower (still standing), eighteen stall roundhouse, stock yard, power house and a substantial yard. It is still a crew change point for trainmen; enginemen run through to Kansas City and Fort Madison. Operations here have been greatly reduced in recent years, and further reductions were implemented in mid-1989. Even so, Marceline is still an interesting place to visit. An overpass just west of the station is a nice photo spot. Santa Fe 2-8-0 2546 and a caboose are displayed in Disney Park near the station—a nice place to let the kids play while you photograph trains. *Above . . .* GP39-2 3653 poses in front of the Marceline station on October 10, 1980. The 2300 h.p. unit was rebuilt in December 1986 as the 3405. *Right . . .* You're leaning out the window of an eastbound freight slowing for a crew change as No. 23, the westbound GRAND CANYON, waits out a station stop. It's May 12, 1969, and in two years Amtrak will relegate the train to history. Passenger service is still available, however, as Amtrak's SOUTHWEST CHIEF stops here daily. *Above: Jim Primm; Disney sign and right: Joe McMillan.*

From Marceline, Santa Fe rails head southwestward through Mendon, mile 360.7, and the former location of Whitham, mile 364.7, where Wabash's Brunswick to Omaha line passed under the main line. Dean Lake, mile 368, also boasted a depot and stock yard at one time. At mile 370, the tracks cross the Grand River and climb gently out of the valley to Bosworth, Missouri, at mile 374.3. *Above . . .* In 1969, Bosworth still had an open agency. *Right . . .* GP20 1146 heads a mixed consist of GP35s and GP20s on an eastbound boxcar train through Bosworth during an afternoon thunderstorm on May 7, 1969. *Below . . .* On a better day later that month, a westbound behind the 1119 crosses over from the south to the north main. *Three photos: Joe McMillan.*

Carrollton, mile 386.4, named for Charles Carroll, a signer of the Declaration of Independence, is the county seat of Carroll County. Befitting its importance, the city received an attractive brick depot—completed in June 1917—which still stands today. The structure is presently used by maintenance of way personnel and has been altered somewhat for that purpose. *Above . . .* GP39-2 3690 and a pair of GP20s wheel westbound pigs through Carrollton on October 4, 1980. On the same day . . . *left . . .* U36C 8757 and mate cross bridge 386.6 over the Wakenda Drainage Ditch with an eastbound. *Three photos: Jim Primm.*

The Santa Fe double tracked its Chicago to Kansas City main line between 1904 and 1915. West of Carrollton, the company took advantage of a portion of Wabash's Kansas City-Moberly route which paralleled the Santa Fe. The Wabash had built through the area in 1868, twenty years before Santa Fe. In 1907, Santa Fe and Wabash entered into a paired track agreement which remains in effect today with Wabash's successor, Norfolk Southern. Paired trackage begins at W. B. Junction (formerly Carrollton Junction), mile 388.7. A tower controlled the switches until it was closed in the summer of 1960 after CTC had rendered the facility obsolete. Between W. B. Jct. and mile 405.5 at Hardin, there are two CTC-controlled main tracks; the north track belongs to Santa Fe, the south to NS. Between mile 405.5 and the end of paired trackage at C. A. Junction (formerly Camden Junction), mile 418.2, there are three main tracks. The north and middle mains are Santa Fe, the south NS. Traffic on the north and middle tracks is controlled by automatic block signals (ABS) and on the south track by CTC.

Above . . . Certainly the most interesting station on the paired trackage was Hardin with its combination tower and office. Prior to the coming of CTC, the tower controlled the crossovers and access to and from the third main track. The depot was still an open agency when photographed in May 1974, but it would be gone shortly.

Steam occasionally comes to the Santa Fe, thanks to railroads such as Norfolk & Western and later, Norfolk Southern. *Top right* . . . Nickel Plate Berkshire 759 pauses on Santa Fe rails at Norborne on May 6, 1969. The big 2-8-4 was powering the 14-car "Golden Spike Centennial Limited" from Harmon, New York to Kansas City. From there, Union Pacific diesels took the special west to Ogden, Utah for the May 10th celebration of the completion of the nation's first transcontinental railroad. Years later, on June 22, 1985 . . . *bottom right* . . . beautifully restored N&W 4-8-4 611 pilots a Kansas City to Moberly excursion out of Hardin. *Station photos and top right: Joe McMillan; bottom right: Jim Primm.*

Missouri Route 10 crosses over the Santa Fe at mile 404.8, just east of Hardin. Though the roadway is narrow, the bridge is a nice vantage point. *Top left* . . . On June 6, 1987, SF30C 9567 speeds out of Hardin with pigs for Chicago. Looking the opposite direction from bridge 404.8 . . . *bottom left* . . . GP20 3005 leads mixed freight west. Note that the south main (Norfork Southern) curves away to the right. Between here and W. B. Junction, the north and south mains have separate rights of way. The track at right is a siding. *Above* . . . A westbound Conrail run-through zips under Route 10 on September 13, 1987. The Rio Grande motor is probably off the C-KCSR coal train and may have been picked up at Chillicothe. *Below* . . . On a June day twenty years ago, U28CG 357 and mates rush No. 99, the SUPER C, out of Hardin. If you look closely you can see the Route 10 overpass and station in the distance. The train is on the north main; the track to the right of it is the middle main. The south main line (NS) is out of the photo to the right. *Two photos left page and above: Jim Primm; below: Joe McMillan.*

Like Carrollton, Henrietta, mile 411.3, has an attractive brick station which is still standing. Henrietta used to be the junction point for the 72.6 mile St. Joseph District which angled northwestward through Richmond, Lawson, Lathrop, Plattsburg, Gower and into St. Joseph. The branch, originally constructed by the Wabash in 1870, at one time extended southeast of Henrietta to North Lexington, Missouri, a distance of 3.2 miles. Matter of fact, Henrietta was once known as Lexington Junction. The Henrietta-North Lexington spur was abandoned and dismantled in 1933. The rest of the branch was abandoned in several stages in the late 1970s. By April 1979, it had been cut back to Richmond, 5 miles out of Henrietta. That segment was abandoned on January 31, 1984. A five track enginehouse was located at Henrietta in the middle of the St. Joseph District wye, and a small yard was located east of the station. The depot was closed in September 1982 and is used today for maintenance of way purposes.

Missouri Route 13 passes over the tracks at the west end of the Henrietta station, providing an interesting photo perspective. To*p left* . . . New DASH 8-40B 7429 speeds by the nice looking station on September 17, 1988. Two months earlier, on July 9th at 6:22 p.m. . . . *bottom left* . . . the camera looks over the depot roof at GP7 2238 hustling train 253 (East Peoria-Kansas City) through town. Shown are the north and middle mains, two sidings and a portion of the old Henrietta yard. The south main track (NS) passes through town to the far right of the photo; a portion of which can be seen to the left of the vertical storage tank. *Above* . . . This is the view from the west side of the Route 13 overpass. It's 10:03 a.m., August 20, 1985, and GP38 2343, fresh from remanufacturing at Cleburne shops, leads an eastbound on the middle main. *Below* . . . Norfolk Southern train 383 speeds westbound auto racks by milepost 414X, 8.6 miles west of Henrietta, on the south main, 5:54 p.m., July 9, 1988. *Top left: Jim Primm; bottom left and below: Joe McMillan; above: Dave Oroszi.*

Camden, Missouri, mile 416.9, is a small town located on paired Santa Fe-Norfolk Southern trackage 11.5 miles west of Henrietta. Its depot was closed in February 1957 and its name has not appeared in the timetable for years. *Above* . . . It's a hot September morning in 1969 as N&W 1940, 1908 and 1936 (U30B/U28B/U30B) curve through town on the north main with westbound autos and autoparts. The south track lies just out of the photo at right. Coming the opposite direction a decade later . . . *top right* . . . Santa Fe U23B 6326 leads eastbound pigs. Unfortunately, the picturesque building at right has been razed. At C. A. Junction, mile 418.2, the Santa Fe and Norfolk Southern part company. At mile 419 . . . *bottom right* . . . Santa Fe rails pass over the NS main track on a 92-foot skewed, deck girder bridge. On August 30, 1987, B23-7 6355 crosses the structure enroute to Kansas City. *Above: Joe McMillan; two photos right page: Jim Primm.*

The Missouri River bridge at Sibley is an impressive structure. The original crossing was completed during the first half of 1888. Increasing engine and train weights soon made replacing the bridge imperative. The November 1915 issue of *The Santa Fe Magazine* said that the old bridge "...owing to its light and faulty construction, had become unsafe for the heavy equipment and traffic sent over it. For some years large engines have not been allowed to work steam while crossing its long spans, the trains being pushed across by pushers attached on the approaches to the bridge." In September 1911, the company began to replace the superstructure under traffic, a process that lasted until March 1914. *Left* . . . SF30C 9534 rumbles off the west end of the Missouri River bridge in September 1987. Note the rear of the train at right on the high approach fill. *Above* . . . On August 29, 1987, long-nose SD40-2 5135 leads a string of pigs across two of the three large deck trusses on the east end of the bridge. The Missouri Public Service Company's Sibley generating plant, which Santa Fe serves, is partially visible behind the nearest bridge pier. *Right* . . . A caboose trails eastbound freight high on the east approach viaduct in June 1988. *Three photos: Jim Primm.*

The present bridge is 4,057 feet long and carries the tracks 100 feet above the river. While the old bridge was a single track structure, this one was built with gauntlet track. In a gauntlet arrangement, one track overlaps the other where clearances are insufficient for two separate tracks. The gauntlet was later removed, however, and single track was restored. The most impressive features of the crossing are the three 396-foot through trusses, the 2,000-foot east approach viaduct and the 10,000-foot east approach fill which reaches a height of 65 feet at its highest point.

SD40-2 5045 eases an eastbound over the bridge at the maximum speed allowed, 30 m.p.h. The date is August 13, 1978. *Photo: Jim Primm.*

Top left . . . *A plea*sant morning in May 1980 finds month-old B23-7 6401 and four leased Chessie units approaching the west end of the Missouri River bridge. The two main tracks become one immediately behind the photographer. From bridge 427.2 . . . *bottom left* . . . the camera catches a string of Geeps pulling coal empties out of the Missouri Public Service generating station in August 1977. The empties will return to Kansas City for interchange to the Frisco. Currently, Union Pacific unit trains of Illinois coal come to the Santa Fe at Eton, Missouri, mile 436.5, 9.8 miles west of Sibley. Santa Fe crews handle the train to the generating station, unload it and return the empties to the UP. An attractive wood frame station and tower combination was built at Sibley when the Missouri River bridge was rebuilt. It had a sixteen-lever interlocking machine to control operations over the gauntlet track. The depot was torn down in the mid-1960s; it was replaced in March 1964 by a small station moved there from Gower, Missouri (on the abandoned Henrietta-St. Joseph branch). It still stands in 1989, used as a tool house by maintenance of way forces. *Above* . . . A trio of immaculate SDFP45s sail past the structure on May 25, 1983 with a director's special returning to Chicago. Seven years earlier at the same location . . . *below* . . . Bicentennial SD45-2 5701 and an F45 team up to power a string of mechanical reefers east in a scene that cannot be repeated. The last two Santa Fe mechanical reefers on the roster were sold for scrap in April 1988. (A few cars, however, could still be seen in 1989 assigned to maintenance of way service.) The Santa Fe painted SD45-2s 5700-5704 in this patriotic scheme between February 1975 and January 1976 to help celebrate the nation's 200th birthday. The 5701 returned to its standard colors in April 1977 and was converted to cabless booster 5514 at San Bernardino shops in December 1987. *Four photos: Jim Primm.*

Top . . . Bridge 427.8, just west of Sibley, provides an autumn view of SD40-2 5143 on an eastbound in October 1988. U33C 8501 and mates . . . *left* . . . enter double track territory at the west end of the Missouri River bridge at Sibley. The track curving off to the left is the Missouri Public Service balloon track used to turn and unload unit coal trains. *Above* . . . The Atherton "depot" in May 1974. *Top and left: Jim Primm; above: Joe McMillan.*

Santa Fe rails cross the Little Blue River at mile 431.6, just east of Atherton. On October 4, 1987 ... *above* ... eastbound C30-7 8144 crosses the Little Blue on a 149-foot through truss. *Below* ... Nine years earlier, in September 1978, B23-7 6358 leads a westbound across 420 feet of trestle at the west end of the structure. *Both photos: Jim Primm.*

The Union Pacific—formerly the Missouri Pacific—has trackage rights over the Santa Fe between Eton and Congo, a distance of 7.7 miles. *Above* . . . On June 28, 1980, an eastbound Missouri Pacific train rounds the curve at Eton and prepares to leave Santa Fe rails for MoPac's River Subdivision (Kansas City to Jefferson City via Boonville). Note the ex-Rock Island unit sandwiched between B23-7 4650 (with license plate hanging on its nose) and the GP7.

Sugar Creek is located at mile 442.6 and is the site of a large Amoco refinery. Once a very busy station, Sugar Creek currently sees little activity, except on the main line. *Top left* . . . GP30 3229 rounds the curve in front of the depot on a late afternoon in May 1974 with a westbound. Thirteen years later . . . *bottom left* . . . U36C 8738 rounds the same curve with eastbound pigs. That's the Amoco refinery on the left. *Top left: Joe McMillan; bottom left and above: Jim Primm.*

Above . . . Brand new B23-7 6365 approaches mile 442, just east of Sugar Creek, with a westbound. The Missouri Portland Cement Company at Courtney is in the background. A few minutes later . . . *top right . . .* the same train ducks under the signal bridge at Congo, mile 444. *Bottom right . . .* For many years, GP7 2899—formerly 99—was assigned to the Sugar Creek local. The train originated at Kansas City's Argentine yard and served industries east of Sheffield. Geep 99 was built at EMD in March 1954 from parts from a wrecked Santa Fe FTA. It was initially rated at 1350 h.p., but was later re-engined with a standard 1500 h.p. 16-567B prime mover. The unit was renumbered 2899 in January 1970 and remanufactured at Cleburne shops in mid-1981, rolling out as low-nose 2013. Since rebuilding, the 2013 has been assigned as a switcher at Chicago's Corwith yard. On October 28, 1978, however, the unique locomotive was speeding the Sugar Creek local west at mile 442. *Three photos: Jim Primm.*

From Congo to Kansas City Terminal Tower 9, Rock Creek Junction, (0.7 mile), the Union Pacific and Santa Fe share paired trackage; Santa Fe owns the north main and UP the south. Both tracks are CTC controlled allowing traffic to flow in either direction on either track. Santa Fe trains travel the north track in both directions, but they can operate over the south track if the need arises. If a westbound Santa Fe were routed over the south track, it would veer away from the north main at Congo, drop down and join UP's Sedalia Subdivision (St. Louis-Kansas City via Sedalia) at Rock Creek Junction, cross under the north track, curve off the UP through KCT's Blue River yard back to the original right of way at KCT Tower 8, Sheffield, mile 446.4. It sounds more complicated than it is, but dispatchers prefer not to run Santa Fe trains that way.

Above . . . GP20 3173 (later 3073) passes milepost 444 at Congo with Kansas City-bound pigs. The right track is the south main; UP ownership—at the time, Missouri Pacific—begins beyond a set of crossovers behind the photographer. *Top right* . . . Three TP&W motors and a Santa Fe Geep pass KCT's Sheffield Tower in November 1980. Trailing the consist are three new Santa Fe B23-7s being delivered to Argentine Shop where they will be set up for service. *Bottom, far right* . . . You're on the Forest Avenue overpass in downtown Kansas City viewing U25B 6604 leading eastbound freight through the "concrete canyon," which runs about two miles from mile 449 to just east of Union Station. *Right* . . . Signs bearing both Santa Fe and KCT mileages were installed recently to physically identify the beginning of speed restrictions and other locations referenced in special instructions, bulletins and circulars. *Four photos: Jim Primm.*

Santa Fe trains operate over the tracks of the Kansas City Terminal Company for a distance of 6.7 miles; from KCT's Sheffield Tower to Santa Fe Junction, west of Union Station (USKC). The old Kansas City Union Depot was located in the "West Bottoms," about three miles northwest of the present site of USKC. The terminal was inconveniently located for several railroads and subject to flooding from the nearby Missouri River. Santa Fe passenger trains would leave the east-west main line at Santa Fe Junction and back the 1.7 miles to Union Depot, a time consuming move. USKC alleviated the inefficiencies associated with Union Depot when it was completed in 1914. It was located on Santa Fe's east-west route and its through tracks greatly expedited the handling of trains. The numbering of Santa Fe mileposts started over again at Union Depot. When USKC was completed, that facility then became the beginning point. Santa Fe Junction was located at mileage 1.7—as measured from the old Union Depot—and that designation was maintained. The distance between the new USKC and Santa Fe Junction was measured, then subtracted from 1.7, which resulted in USKC being designated mile 0.34. An engineering "equation" at the center line of USKC states that "mile 451.17 equals mile 0.34."

Freight trains pass by the north side of the station. *Left* . . . Merger red SF30C 9532 moves west on KCT trackage just east of USKC on December 3, 1988, as viewed from Washington Square Park. From the Main Street overpass on the same day . . . *right* . . . ex-TP&W GP38-2s 2375 and 2378 bracket GP7 2004 enroute from Santa Fe's Argentine Yard to Armco Steel (on KCT) with several cars of scrap. Looking west from the same vantage point . . . *below* . . . the 3558 and 8514 (GP38/U33C) pull eastbound freight by USKC in May 1979. Note the Rock Island train entering the photo at right. *Three photos: Jim Primm.*

Kansas City's Union Station was a magnificent structure when it opened on October 30, 1914. Today, it is mostly derelict and abandoned. Several attempts have been made to redevelop the building, but to no avail. The train sheds and all 18 through tracks under the station concourse have been removed. In 1984, Amtrak moved out of the station to a new track level facility. Passenger trains now arrive and depart on three tracks north of the concourse.

Top left . . . In better days, Santa Fe No. 211, THE TULSAN, prepares for a 6:05 p.m. departure. Trailing U28CG 356 are a baggage car and three coaches, typical for the train at the time. *Bottom left* . . .The next day, August 22, 1968, No. 212, the eastbound TULSAN, approaches USKC on time at 12:10 p.m. Eastbound passengers on board will connect with No. 24, which will arrive in 45 minutes. The TULSANS were discontinued with the coming of Amtrak in May 1971. KCT 52 switches at right.

Probably the best train watching location in Kansas City is on the Missouri-Kansas state line at Santa Fe Junction, 1.36 miles west of USKC. Trains of most railroads serving Kansas City can be seen moving through here. KCT Tower 3 once controlled the junction switches and signals, but it was closed a number of years ago. It still stands in 1989, but it is used only to house signal equipment. *Above* . . . GP39-2 3692 and GP20 3022 lead eastbound freight through the junction in September 1980 while a transfer rumbles by enroute to Argentine Yard. *Right* . . . Also in September 1980, B23-7 6394 moves under the KCT "high line" at Santa Fe Junction with a westbound. The high line provided Union Pacific and Rock Island passenger trains a direct route to Union Station from the west. A recent addition to the bridge provides UP with a connection to Missouri-Kansas-Texas Railroad's Glen Park Yard. (Ownership of the Katy was assumed by Union Pacific in 1988.) *Two photos left page: Joe McMillan; above and right: Jim Primm.*

Above . . . On May 29, 1983, a pair of Geeps grind toward the BN at a point just south of the Hannibal Bridge over the Missouri River. GP7 2059 has just been remanufactured at Cleburne; it was formerly high-nose 2782. *Top left* . . .GP9s 2246 and 2250 wind through the West Bottoms with a transfer for the Burlington Northern. The crew has just set out a cut of cars at the Chicago, Missouri & Western and, in the distance, is seen passing KCT Tower 2 (Old Union Depot Interlocking), which has been closed, but still houses signal and communication equipment. *Bottom left* . . . A year later, a pair of GP9s—2250 and 2245—lead another BN transfer through the same area. Geep 2250 was one of only two GP9s painted in the merger red scheme. (The 2291 was the other.) Cleburne shops gave the 2250 its bright look in February 1986. The vacant area beyond the train (above the second unit) is the site of the old Union Depot. The building itself was located along Union Avenue (seen in the background leading up to the ramp at the right of the train). The station tracks ran roughly from Santa Fe Street to St. Louis Avenue. The first "union station" was built here in 1869, but it was damaged by fire six years later and torn down. The Union Depot was built in 1878 on the same site, but by 1890 it had become badly congested, unable to accommodate the new railroads building into the city. The flood of 1903 nearly destroyed the facility and hastened plans for a new Union Station at a safer and more convenient location. *Three photos: Jim Primm.*

Top left . . . Former TP&W GP38-2s 2378 and 2375 curve off the Hannibal Bridge over the Missouri River in January 1989 with a transfer from BN's North Kansas City yard. At one time, motor vehicles crossed the river on the structure's top deck. The two through girder spans at the near end of the bridge (under the locomotives) pass over several tracks, including Union Pacific's main line linking Neff Yard in North Kansas City, Missouri—formerly Missouri Pacific—with Armstrong Yard in Kansas City, Kansas. *Bottom left . . .* GP7s 2673 and 2722 (later remanufactured to low-nose 2019 and 2227, respectively) move east out of Argentine Yard with a transfer. The Kansas River flows by at right. *Above . . .* In North Kansas City, Missouri, GP9 2250 and mate pause with a Kansas City Southern transfer as a crew member phones the yardmaster at KCS's Knoche Yard for a track in which to leave the cars. The date is April 24, 1988. *Three photos: Jim Primm.*

Above . . . GE U30CGs 8000 and 8002 ease a westbound into Argentine Yard at AY Tower, mile 3.8, on April 11, 1977. Because of a bridge repair project at Sibley, the train was detoured over the Norfolk & Western; it returned to home rails at Santa Fe Junction. A year earlier, transfer locomotives 1419L and 1419A . . . *below* . . . pull a string of cars along the Kansas River east of Argentine Yard. Santa Fe owned two EMD TR-4 "cow and calf" sets built in 1950 and 1951 as the 2418L-2418A and 2419L-2419A, respectively. The units were renumbered 1418L-1418A and 1419L-1419A in 1974 and remanufactured in 1979, emerging as 1242-1243 and 1244-1245. Both sets were off the roster by mid-1985. *Two Photos: Jim Primm.*

Above . . . The main line along Santa Fe's 5th Street Yard in Kansas City, Kansas (mile 2), was a busy place on February 1, 1981. Leading the nearest westbound is SD45 5497, making one of its first runs on the east end of the railroad after having been remanufactured by Morrison-Knudsen at Boise, Idaho, two months prior. The 5497 was one of four SD45s rebuilt by M-K (5496-5499) with 3600 h.p., 16-cylinder Sulzer prime movers. The Sulzer engines didn't work out and were replaced by EMD 20-cylinder engines at San Bernardino between December 1984 and July 1985. At that time the units were renumbered 5405-5408, respectively. Note the high line in the background running across the "bottoms" to the upper deck of the Kansas River bridge at left. As mentioned earlier, the elevated trackage provided Union Pacific and Rock Island passenger trains access to Union Station. Freight trains still use the structure, though most travel a surface route and cross the river on the lower bridge deck. Santa Fe Junction lies just out of the photo where the trains curve out of sight. *Photo: Jim Primm.*

Above . . . Bicentennial SD45-2 5700 leads one of the last westbound Super C's into the afternoon sun on a beautiful day in May 1976. The 5700's reign over Santa Fe's most prestigious train was soon to end. The 3600 h.p. unit was repainted to standard blue and yellow warbonnet paint a year later, and converted to booster unit 5517 in January 1988. Santa Fe's 5th Street yard, shown at left, has been used for years to store cars. Using the 12th Street bridge as a vantage point . . . *top right* . . . the photographer catches a pair of GP38-2s (ex-TP&W) leading a transfer from the BN in January 1989 (see photo top of page 180). The 7th Street bridge crosses the Kansas River in the distant background. From 12th Street a month earlier . . . *bottom right* . . . the photographer records the same consist leaving Argentine with another transfer. The 18th Street bridge is in the distance; it passes over the east end of the yard and shop area. AY Tower is located at the foot of the tall light tower around the curve. *Three photos: Jim Primm.*

Above . . . GP38-2 2375 (ex-TP&W 2006) rumbles along the Kansas River east of AY Tower at 12th Street in December 1988. *Top right* . . . It's May 3, 1980 as month-old B23-7 6401 and mates pause at AY Tower while the crew obtains their orders before backing down to their train. The overhead bridge behind the consist is 18th Street. *Bottom right* . . . This view looks east off the Goddard Avenue overpass, mile 4.7. The engineer of merger red SD45 5338 pilots the consist toward his train at the west end of the yard. The tall building beyond the power house smoke stacks in the middle of the photo is the Argentine diesel shop—now officially labeled Argentine Locomotive Maintenance and Inspection Terminal (LMIT)— which was built in 1954, and added to several times since. The metal building to its right (with the three doors) is the new DSF (Diesel Service Facility), completed in 1982 and modified in 1987. The DSF is a large indoor servicing facility where locomotives are inspected, fueled, lubed and sanded. The units in the background are waiting servicing or call to duty. *Three photos: Jim Primm.*

Above . . . Santa Fe's fleet of U28CGs and U30CG's was at the Argentine diesel shop on April 19, 1969; half the units are shown in this lineup. The colorful GEs were being removed from passenger service at the time and were being setup for freight duties. Several derailments attributed to the locomotives prompted Santa Fe to take the action. *Below . . .* F3A 22 and F7A 250C wait on the ready tracks under 18th Street in 1969. Both units were subsequently rebuilt to CF7s: 22—later renumbered 308C—to 2554 in September 1973, and 250C to 2582 in February 1973. The 2554 was scrapped in 1983 and the 2582 was sold to a switching contractor in Beaumont, Texas in June 1986. *Two photos: Joe McMillan.*

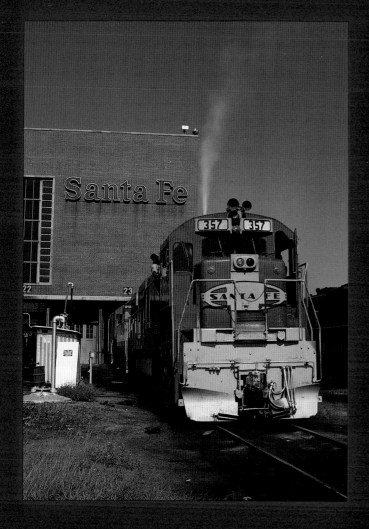

Left . . . U28CG 357 undergoes inspection at Argentine on August 21, 1968. F7A 347C and U36C 8721 idle away the hours in front of the diesel shop in August 1973 . . . *below*. The 347C was built as the 39C in September 1949. It was renumbered to 306C in April 1971 when assigned to Amtrak trains operating on the Santa Fe. In 1973, new Amtrak SDP40Fs began bumping Santa Fe F-units from passenger service. As the units were released, the company began shopping them for freight service. In this photo, the 306C has just been renumbered 347C. In a few days its red nose will be painted yellow, complete with blue nose emblem. Santa Fe selected the 347C for preservation in 1975 and moved it to Albuquerque for storage. In early 1986, the 347C, along with Santa Fe's entire collection of preserved locomotives, was donated to the California State Railroad Museum at Sacramento. In February 1988, the 347C and booster 347B were moved to San Bernardino and repainted red/silver warbonnet. While not restored to operating condition, these units have nevertheless starred at several rail displays and celebrations. *Left: Joe McMillan; below: Jim Primm.*

Above . . . A winter morning in December 1981 finds Santa Fe, TP&W and Milwaukee Road units idling under 18th Street. The Milwaukee Road was running a train into Argentine at the time and its power would lay over at the facility until ready to return. The TP&W units were in run-through service between Kansas City and East Peoria. Ironically, TP&W 2006 would later become Santa Fe 2375 and be assigned to transfer service out of this yard. *Below* . . . On March 27, 1976, the late afternoon sun lights the colorful nose of bicentennial 5703 on the point of train 198, the SUPER C, while a switcher adds cars to the rear of the train. The SUPER ran until May 1976. *Two photos: Jim Primm.* **End.**

Acknowledgements

McMillan Publications is excited about bringing you the **Santa Fe in Color Series**. Naturally, a project such as this cannot be done without the help of many people. While there are a number who deserve mention, we particularly want to thank Jim Primm who has been working with us on this project for several years.

A special thanks also goes to Mike Blaszak who provided photos, wrote the foreword, proofread the text and assisted in researching caption material. Appreciation goes to Mike and Mark Danneman for the excellent end-sheet map. And, of course, we are especially indebted to the photographers whose names appear with their photos.

Lastly, a special appreciation is expressed to our Apple Macintosh computer which showed us an entirely new way to efficiently lay out books.

HIGH GREEN TO MARCELINE
By Joe McMillan

PUBLISHED BY:
McMillan Publications, Inc., Woodridge, Illinois

BOOK LAYOUT AND DESIGN
Joe McMillan

DUSTJACKET DESIGN AND ADVERTISING
Alan Barrett Graphic Design, Sacramento, California

TYPESETTING AND FILM NEGATIVES
The Image Center, Michigan City, Indiana

COLOR SEPARATIONS AND IMAGE ASSEMBLY
Jim Walter Color Separations, Beloit, Wisconsin

PRINTING
Winnebago Color Press, Menasha, Wisconsin

BINDING
Zonne Bookbinders, Inc., Chicago, Illinois

KANSAS CITY DETAIL

KANSAS CITY
KANSAS

Turner

Kansas River

Armourdale

Argentine Yard

Argentine Engine Terminal

To Los Angeles

UP

SSW RI

AT&SF

KCS

KCT

SSW RI

UP

KCT

AT&SF

BN SLSF

(C&NW)
UP MP

Missouri River

BN

BN

NS N&W

KCS

UP MP

KCS

SOO MILW

KCT

KCS

SOO MILW

AT&SF
UP MP

KCS

CM&W ICG

BN Hannibal Bridge

Old Union Depot

KANSAS CITY

Union Station

Santa Fe Jct.
AT&SF 5th St. Yard

Sheffield Jct.

Rock Creek Jct.

Congo Jct.

To Chicago

BN SLSF

KCS

MISSOURI

IOWA

Orme

Ponemah

Smithshire 201.

Media 204.6

Stronghurst 208.9

Decorra 212.4

Lomax 218.9

Niota 224.8

Dallas City 224.8

Fort Madison 234.3

New Boston 244.0

Argyle 248.0

Dumas 252.3

Revere 256.0

Medill 263.1

Wyaconda 272.3

Gorin 277.6

Baring 290.7

Hurdland 300.1

Gibbs 306.4

La Plata 312.7

Elmer 322.9

Ethel 329.7

Hart 336.0

Bucklin 341.5

Marceline 347.3

Rothville 354.6

Mendon 360.7

Whitham 364.7

Dean Lake 368.1

Bosworth 374.3

Carrollton 386.4

Richmond 5.1

W.B. Jct. 388.7

Norborne 396.6

Hardin 405.4

Henrietta 411.3

N. Lexington

C.A. Jct. 418.2

Floyd 421.7

Sibley 426.7

Atherton 434.0

Eton 436.5

Sugar Creek 442.6

Congo 444.2

Sheffield

KANSAS CITY 461.4

Santa Fe Jct. 1.7 451.1

Argentine 4.8

To Los Angeles

St. Joseph

Plattsburg 43.8

Lathrop 35.7

Former Santa Fe
St. Joseph District

Lawson 24.8

AT&SF

AT&SF

**KANSAS CITY
DETAIL
SEE ABOVE**

TP&W

La H

KJ

Keokuk

KJ

Ferris

Warsaw

KJ

Hamilton

SantaFe

MISSOURI

KANSAS

To Los Angeles

0	10	20	30	40	50

MILES

AT&SF **ATCHISON, TOPEKA & SANTA FE**
B&OCT **B&O CHICAGO TERMINAL**
BRC **BELT RAILWAY OF CHICAGO**
BN **BURLINGTON NORTHERN**
C&NW **CHICAGO & NORTH WESTERN**
C&WI **CHICAGO & WESTERN INDIANA**
CB&Q **CHICAGO, BURLINGTON & QUINCY**
CC&P **CHICAGO, CENTRAL & PACIFIC**
CM&W **CHICAGO, MISSOURI & WESTERN**
CSS&SB **SOUTH SHORE**
CR **CONRAIL**

CSX **CSX TRANSPORTATION**
EJ&E **ELGIN, JOLIET & EASTERN**
GTW **GRAND TRUNK WESTERN**
IC **ILLINOIS CENTRAL**
ICG **ILLINOIS CENTRAL GULF**
IHB **INDIANA HARBOR BELT**
IAIS **IOWA INTERSTATE**
KCS **KANSAS CITY SOUTHERN**
KCT **KANSAS CITY TERMINAL**
KJ **KEOKUK JUNCTION**
METRA **METROPOLITAN RAIL CORP.**

MILW **MILWAUKEE ROAD**
MP **MISSOURI PACIFIC**
NS **NORFOLK SOUTHERN**
N&W **NORFOLK & WESTERN**
PRR **PENNSYLVANIA**
RI **ROCK ISLAND**
SLSF **FRISCO**
SSW **COTTON BELT**
SOO **SOO LINE**
TP&W **TOLEDO, PEORIA & WESTERN**
UP **UNION PACIFIC**

MAP BY MIKE DANNEMAN AND MARK DANNEMAN